"Ameri captures the innocence and vulnerability of childhood…
and the growth of a defiant, independent young adult…Get ready
to rethink what you thought it was like to grow up in the Arab
world in the 1950s and 1960s."

—Evelyn Alsultany, University of Michigan,
author of *Arabs and Muslims in the Media*

"Twenty-three vignettes spanning three decades…in Amman,
Damascus and Jerusalem… Ameri's free, rebellious spirit permeates
these pages…"

—Raja Shehadeh, author, lawyer, human rights activist

"Ameri's unusual memoir…enchants us with witty, subtle humor…
The worsening political crises through which she lived are exposed
through ordinary stages in her life. This volume is slim, but what it
conveys is immense."

—Elaine C. Hagopian, Simmons College

"An endearing and intimate autobiography…"

—Salim Tamari, Georgetown University

THE SCENT OF JASMINE

COMING OF AGE IN JERUSALEM AND DAMASCUS

ANAN AMERI

OLIVE
BRANCH
PRESS

An imprint of Interlink Publishing Group, Inc.
www.interlinkbooks.com

To my parents, Um Arwa and Abu Arwa,
and to the amazing women in my life.

~

First published in 2017 by
Olive Branch Press
An imprint of
Interlink Publishing Group, Inc.
46 Crosby Street, Northampton, MA 01060
www.interlinkbooks.com

Library of Congress Cataloging-in-Publication Data

Names: Ameri, Anan, author.
Title: The scent of jasmine : coming of age in Jerusalem and Damascus / by Anan
    Ameri.
Description: Northampton MA : Olive Branch Press, 2017. | Includes
    bibliographical references.
Identifiers: LCCN 2017009133 | ISBN 9781566560016
Subjects: LCSH: Ameri, Anan. | Palestinian Arabs--West Bank--Biography. |
    Palestinian Arabs--Syria--Damascus--Biography.
Classification: LCC DS126.6.A53 A3 2017 | DDC 305.892/740092 [B] --dc23
LC record available at https://lccn.loc.gov/2017009133

Printed and bound in the United States of America

CONTENTS

Introduction

I was born in Damascus to a Syrian mother and Palestinian father in the fall of 1944. I lived in the cities of Jerusalem and Damascus, Amman, Cairo and Beirut. Then in 1974, at the age of thirty, my life journey took me to a new world, where I lived and worked in Detroit, Washington, DC, and Cambridge, Massachusetts, finally settling in Ann Arbor, Michigan.

For over forty years, I worked with immigrant communities in the US, mostly from the Arab World. Their voices made me appreciate how we are constantly trying to recreate, reconstruct and tell the stories of who we are, and to figure out how our individual stories are part of larger ones. Inevitably, their stories led me back to my own. As I recall and reflect on my early life story before coming to this country, I realize how much it mirrors enormous changes that were taking place in the Arab world.

On one hand, I feel lucky to have grown up, and come of age, when many Arab countries enjoyed a certain level of openness and acceptance. It was an exciting era of liberation movements, nationalism, and international solidarity. But I am less lucky to have been born in 1944, only a few years before the erasure of my homeland from all maps, when our family, along with another 850,000 Palestinians, became refugees. In spite of my young age, those events forever formed me, emotionally and psychologically. To a greater extent, they influenced many of the most important choices in my life.

As a child, I used to fantasize about being Swiss or Norwegian, not because I wanted to be blond or rich but because I wished to be free from fears of disaster, separation and sadness, and from seeing my father, his friends and relatives forever grieving their loss of Palestine. At the same time, I was drawn to their passionate political discussions. Their vivid conversations, personal anecdotes and stories ignited my curiosity and imagination.

But my childhood wasn't anywhere near as dark or serious as it might sound. I was fortunate to have a Syrian extended family on my mother's side, who gave me the security and stability that my own parents, with their displacement and constant moves, were unable to provide. I was also fortunate to be born to parents who gave me space to grow, taught me to be independent and instilled in me compassion for those who are less fortunate. Both of my parents were socially and politically liberal. And while they hardly ever agreed on anything, they were both determined to give their four children the best education possible. They expected their three daughters to chart their own futures.

Perhaps the most telling thing about my parents is their names. Unlike the tradition in our region, where a father and mother are known by the name of their firstborn son, my parents were known as Abu Arwa and Um Arwa—father and mother of Arwa—after my sister, their daughter and firstborn. Occasionally, someone would call my father Abu Ayman, after his only son, and my baba would kindly respond, "I am Abu Arwa. She is the one who made me a father."

My parents were by no means wealthy, but what we lacked in material luxury was compensated for by a large circle of family and friends, and a rich social life. Although very different from each other, my father and mother each provided me with a set of values that guided me. My aunts, on both sides of my family, were strong and determined. My mother, the youngest of nine children, was exceptionally intelligent and independent. She graduated from college, traveled on her own and spoke her mind. She owned her own business—a print shop in downtown Amman—managed an all-male staff and worked well into her mid-seventies. Mother enjoyed a network of professional friends, including political activists, artists and poets. These women, each of whom I called *Khalto*, or Auntie, never used terms like women's liberation or feminism, but they did teach me, at a fairly young age, that the sky was the limit when it came to my education and career choices.

My father loved to read and write. He published numerous books and articles, and was well respected, not only for his intellect but more so for his honesty and integrity. Although known as a socialist, he held many high-level positions in the Jordanian government, including Minister of Foreign Affairs, Minister of Education, and Ambassador to Egypt, reflecting a time when a diversity of political affiliations was more tolerated, in spite of periodic repression of the press and political opposition.

After leaving East Jerusalem in 1950 when I was about six, my childhood was spent traveling back and forth between Amman and Damascus. My maternal grandfather, a rich merchant born in 1862, owned a large, beautiful home in the Old City of Damascus, centrally located and close to two historical landmarks—the Umayyad Mosque and Souq al-Hamadyeh. My grandfather, whose life spanned nearly a full century, embodied many contradictions, as he tried to cope with the rapidly changing world around him. Liberal enough to send two of his daughters to college in Beirut in the early 1900s, he also expected all of his children and grandchildren to line up and kiss his hand every time he entered the house. On the other hand, my father was secular, and never practiced any religion. This was neither praised nor denounced, not even by my religious grandfather. My maternal uncle was politically conservative, but he and my father enjoyed each other's company and laughed together, especially when they shared a glass of whiskey.

My adolescence, as well as that of my generation, which came of age in the 1960s, was the product of that era. Just like the sixties in the US, in the Arab world we had our own sixties. While on the surface the issues might seem different, they were actually similar. In the US, the sixties centered on the Vietnam War, the Civil Rights movement, and women's rights; in the Arab world, we rebelled against male-dominated societies, colonialism, and oppressive regimes. We rallied for women's liberation and, of course, for the liberation of Palestine.

I grew up in a Muslim culture, but I never even knew if I was a Sunni or Shi'a until I became an adult. Our friends, teachers, neighbors and local store owners were mixed, religiously and ethnically. Mango Street in Amman, where I lived between 1952 and

1968, was home to Christians and Muslims, Jordanians, Palestinians, Syrians and Lebanese, as well as Armenians, Circassians, Chechens and Assyrians. We were all neighbors and friends. We went to the same schools, played together, and never gave much thought to our differences or thought in terms of "us" versus "them."

Although the Arab world I grew up in was hardly democratic, and had its own challenges, during the 1950s and 1960s there were numerous political parties and unions, and we felt the promise of a better tomorrow. Those years also witnessed political unrest and military coups, which were followed by the detentions of political opposition. In 1958, the Jordanian government arrested my father because of his socialist beliefs. In 1966, the Syrian Baath regime arrested my conservative uncle. For my own political activism, I was kicked out of school and university. But compared to the intolerance we see now, those days seem like heaven.

A few years ago, while sharing with my niece how most of our hopes and dreams had been crushed, she said, "At least your generation had hope." When her generation surprised us with the "Arab Spring," their revolution was co-opted and crushed, along with their dreams for a brighter future.

~

In 1993, I resigned from my job as director of the Palestine Aid Society of America, a position I had held since 1980, not knowing what to do next. All I knew was that my body and soul were aching, begging me to take mercy on them. It was a low point in my life. I was totally exhausted and demoralized, not from being overworked and underpaid but from feeling defeated on all fronts: defeated by lack of progress on the Palestinian front, a cause I had dedicated most of my adult life to; defeated by the tragedy of the 1991 US war in Iraq; defeated by my failed marriage to a man I respected and loved dearly. It was also a time when I was approaching my fiftieth birthday, a time of midlife crisis. Some handle it by buying a new red convertible; others find a lover. I took a sabbatical.

The only decision I made when I resigned from the Palestine Aid Society was not to jump into another job for at least a year. I wanted to take my time to figure out what the next chapter of my life would look like. During that year I spent a lot of time contemplating what makes us who we are, what makes us choose certain paths rather than others, how history, people and relationships shape our destinies. In the process, I began to remember experiences that, in fact, had never left me. *The Scent of Jasmine* was conceived during that year but didn't see the light of day until twenty-some years later.

While recollecting and reflecting on these experiences, some images became especially vivid, as if they had happened yesterday. My first memory of 1948, when I wasn't yet four years old, came back to haunt me: the nightly bombing, my puppies, my father wrapping his warm arms around me, and my mother getting smaller and smaller as I looked at her from the backseat window of my uncle's car while he drove us away to safety.

I began to remember my family's lively conversations and stories, to reimagine and relive significant episodes of my past, reconstructing forgotten facts.

In my apartment in Washington, DC, I spent hours writing. As I jotted down one story, another would invade my brain and I would write it down, as well. I discovered the healing power of writing, of returning to events, moments and individuals that had left their mark on me. I came to realize that my strong, fearless mother, whom I had fought and resented for not being like my friends' stay-at-home mothers, had to a great extent made me and my two sisters the independent women we had become.

~

During my childhood and adolescence, socializing was our main source of entertainment. Family and friends would gather almost daily to exchange news, gossip and remember happy or sad times. In my maternal grandfather's home in the Old City of Damascus, I would see my mother, aunts and uncles sipping coffee, talking and laughing. In the anecdotes I heard in these gatherings, personal incidents often were intertwined with news of larger, or more threatening, events. But this warm tradition of conversational storytelling kept our memories, ties and resilience alive.

As I wrote these stories, I shared some of them with close friends. They encouraged me to keep writing, and I did. I wrote these personal journals to heal, to regroup, to understand, without thinking of any end product.

Most of these twenty-three vignettes in this short volume were first written during that year of 1993. Many were written from my voice and perspective as a child or young person. One of the last stories was written first, in 1991, in response to the first US war against Iraq. When I got a new job as the founding director of the Arab American National Museum, I shoved all these papers into a drawer. For more than twenty years they sat there, collecting dust. But in many ways, they kept me company. Whenever I felt too distressed or discouraged, struggling to create a home for the cultural memory of Arab immigrants, I'd think of the restorative energy of remembering and retelling my own stories, and promise myself to return to them.

In 2014, a year after I retired from my work with the Museum, I retrieved my deteriorating, yellowing pages and started to reread them. I liked most of what was there. A few of the vignettes were sent back to the drawer, with a promise to visit them again later. The rest I edited and rewrote. I also wrote new ones. Gradually, the storytelling voices and images of my early years came back to life, recalling for me the familiar scent of jasmine.

I

1. And They Never Lived Happily Ever After

Amman, 1954

I heard my parents arguing as I descended the few steps that led to our home in Amman. I was only ten years old and was coming from school for lunch. I couldn't figure out what was going on, nor why my father, who usually came home around two o'clock, was already back.

I tiptoed into the house from the side door and froze in the short corridor that led to the dining room where my parents stood facing each other. My heart started to pound as I heard my father screaming.

"The kitchen is a mess! I can't even get myself a glass of water."

When my father saw me, he went to his bedroom and slammed the door. My mother walked reluctantly into the kitchen. I followed her.

Dressed in a red cashmere top, black straight skirt and new high heels, and with her black hair recently cut to the latest fashion, she looked so out of place. She leaned against the kitchen counter staring at all the dirty pots and dishes. I stood by the kitchen door, watching, not knowing what to do. The whole scene looked more like a movie than real life. Moments later she started to cry.

"I hate you Tal'at Jabri. *Allah la yesamhek ya* Suad, may God never forgive you," she said, referring to her father and older sister Suad. "You both talked me into this marriage. Look at me, having to deal with all this mess, as if I am a servant to the Aamirys."

"Please Mama, don't cry. I will clean the kitchen," I said, joining her in crying.

"This Tuffaha," she said, referring to our live-in help, "she told me she was going to visit her family for a week, but she's been gone for almost ten days."

Tuffaha, who was in her late forties, had been living with us for over five years. She was stocky, moved slowly and seemed pained when she had to do certain tasks like mopping the floor or feeding the woodstove. But she was extremely organized and superclean, and that made my father happy. She also knew how to cook, which made my mother happy. Twice a year, Tuffaha would visit her family who lived in a refugee camp in the West Bank. Whenever that happened, I knew trouble was on the way.

"Mama, it's been only four days since Tuffaha left. She left on Thursday and today is only Monday."

"Don't argue with me."

"Sorry, Mama. I'm sure she'll come back soon."

"Your father," she yelled, as if I were responsible for him, "he is such a neat freak. I can't handle it. I hate housework. I hate being married. I never did any work at my parents' house. We always had help."

"I'll help you, Mama. I will."

I was the second child, and my sister Arwa, who is only fifteen months older, hated housework and managed to escape it whenever she could. I also hated housework. But what I hated more were my parents' fights, which were not uncommon; neither were my pathetic attempts to halt them. Whenever my mother got upset with my father, she would curse her own father and older sister Suad for making her marry him. And when she wasn't so upset, she would complain about life in Amman and how much she missed her family, or talk about the wonderful life she had in Damascus before getting married.

To keep my overly dramatic mother happy, we always had live-in help. But whenever the housekeeper took a few days off to visit her own family, or when we were between housekeepers, all hell broke loose. For my mother to take care of a home, four children and a compulsive husband was just a dreadful nightmare. I often wonder if I became a neat freak like my father in order to keep peace in our home, or if it was simply the curse of his genes.

My mother, Siham, was stunningly beautiful. Her tall and slender body moved gracefully, and her fair complexion, green eyes and black hair turned many heads. She was very aware and proud of her elegance and never hesitated to say, "I don't need to wear makeup." In addition to her alluring looks, my mother came from money. Her father, Tal'at Jabri, was an influential merchant, and her family was part of the Damascene elite. She was the youngest of nine kids, the apple of her father's eye and spoiled rotten. When she met my father, she was twenty-one and had just graduated from American Junior College for Women.[1]

My father, Mohammed Adib Aamiry, a Palestinian from Jaffa, came from a more humble middle-class background. He was the oldest of four, and his father died when he was only ten years old. As the firstborn, he felt responsible for the well-being of his siblings, which became much more complicated after 1948. My father was handsome, well-respected and highly educated. He was fourteen years older than my mother, and unlike the social butterfly my mother was, my father enjoyed the serenity of his study and spent many hours in the company of his books.

My worlds-apart parents got married in 1942, and I cannot say that they lived happily ever after.

I have heard so many stories telling how such a strange union possibly could have happened. When I was about eleven, my cousin Nabila, who was four years older than me, explained it this way.

"Khalto Siham was in love with someone my jido and teta did not like. He was a flamboyant poet, and that wasn't the sort of husband they had in mind for their lovely daughter. They talked her into marrying your father."

"I don't believe it," I said. "No one can make Mama do anything she doesn't want to do."

"No, it's true. I even know who Nabila is talking about— Nizar Qabbani, right?" said Arwa, who loved to hang around my older cousins, as she thought they were cool and sophisticated.

"Shut up, Arwa," said Nabila. "You swore not to tell. I'll never tell you anything anymore."

My father had a different story.

"I wanted to marry an educated woman, and my Syrian

neighbors in Salt, the Helwani family, knew your mother's family and led me to her."

My mother's story went like this.

"When I met your father, I felt an immediate attraction because he looked like Gandhi. I was young and foolish."

My cousin Ibtisam, the oldest cousin on my mother's side— only eleven years younger than my mother—claimed to know the ultimate truth.

"Don't listen to any of them. I know the real story. Aunt Suad loved women," she said, referring to my mother's oldest sister. "That's why she never got married. When your father asked for your mother's hand, Nathmiyeh Khanum, Khalto Suad's lover, was living in Salt. She is the one who convinced your mother to marry your father, so she could visit Salt more often."

"What do you mean Khalto Suad loves women?" I asked.

"This is a big secret. Don't tell anyone," said Ibtisam. She made Arwa and me put our hands on the Quran and say "*Wallah*, I swear, I will never say a word."

Maybe the Arabic proverb, *libyoot asrar*, homes are secrets,[2] is true. My mother's family had many secrets, like my jido's relation-ship with his Sudanese servant-slave Saida, whose name ironically means "happy," a relationship that produced my black uncle, Ismat. And there were as many hushed rumors about my adopted cousin Aida—where did she come from, and who were her real parents?

I may never know the real story behind my parents' union. But I do know that for my mother to marry a high school principal with limited income and to live in a humble house in Salt was a big letdown. Even though Salt at the time was the largest city in Jordan, it paled in comparison to cosmopolitan Damascus, where my mother was raised, or to Beirut where she went to college. Throughout my childhood I heard my mother say, "Your father expected me to live in Salt! The house we had was so small, it could easily fit in the upper *qa'ah*, or hall, of my father's home. And Salt! Oh my God, it had nothing, absolutely nothing. He must have been out of his mind to expect me to live there."

Armed with beauty, intelligence and wit, my mother was not going to live in Salt, no matter what.

Before long, my father landed a job in Jerusalem as director of the Arabic section of the Palestine Broadcasting Service radio station, known as *Huna al-Quds*, This is Jerusalem,[3] run by the British who had colonized Palestine at the time. Since the British were much richer than the Jordanians, my father got a better salary. My mother was happy with her husband's big raise and cherished her new life in Jerusalem, although it didn't match up to life in her Damascus.

"The Jerusalemites are classy, *akaber,* but they're not as generous as the Damascene, and they really don't know how to cook," my mother would say.

"Sorry Mama, you don't know how to cook either. You cook the same thing all the time. One day it's rice and green beans, the next day rice and okra, then rice and peas. When you go fancy you cook us chicken and *hasweh,* or *fatet* hummus, and when we have guests over you order food from your cousin's restaurant."

"What's wrong with that?"

"You never make us kibbeh, grape leaves or stuffed *kussa.*"

"That's a waste of time, and I don't like to cook. But I do know good food, and nothing ever tastes like the food at Beit Ahli."

"Of course, nothing in the world is better than at your family's place in Damascus."

"Tell me, when did you ever eat better food or smell nicer scents than at your jido's, especially that jasmine?"

While my mother didn't bring with her the Damascene art of cooking, she definitely brought the scent of jasmine. In all the homes we lived in, Mama always brought a jasmine tree to plant, often by her bedroom window.

My mother was never far from her family, with her cousin Abdo living in Jerusalem and owning a transportation company that ran busses and taxis between Jerusalem and Damascus. She went there whenever she was bored, missed her family and friends or wanted to shop. She also went there when she gave birth to each of her four children, three girls and a boy.

As it turned out, I spent most of my summers and holidays at Beit Jido, my grandfather's house. My mother would send me, along with my three siblings, to her parents' home whenever she was mad at my father or whenever she needed a break from her kids, and both happened a lot. We were also sent there whenever there was a crisis. The longest and most memorable was during the 1948 Palestinian-Israeli war, when my parents were forced out of their home in the west side of Jerusalem. The other long stay was in 1958, after a military coup in Iraq, which toppled the Royal family. King Hussein of Jordan, a first cousin of the deposed Iraqi royalty, declared a state of emergency and arrested thousands of people, including my father because of his socialist ideology.

My mother, Siham Tala't Jabri, and my father, Mohammed Adib Aamiry, in Amman, Jordan, in 1956, with jasmine tree in the background.

2. EARLY LESSONS OF SEPARATION

Jerusalem, spring 1948

On the west side of Jerusalem came my first awareness of home:[4] a bedroom I shared with my sister Arwa; Baba's gentle embrace as I snuck into his warm side of the bed in the early morning or after his afternoon nap; the aroma of orange peel placed on top of a woodstove; and the salon, a large room in the middle of the house, with no doors or windows to the outside. In winter, the salon was our family room and playroom. It also became our shelter, where the six of us—parents, children and puppies—found refuge when the shelling made my heart want to escape my body and my salty tears stung my cheeks.

After leaving the city of Salt, my parents seemed to settle nicely in Jerusalem. With a well-paying job, a spacious house, a big yard and two daughters, they failed to imagine what life might have in store for them. They got my sister Arwa and me two puppies. We named them Lulu and Murjan. Lulu was white and Murjan was light brown. They were fluffy. Their soft hair tickled my face. My greatest joy was when I learned how to make them chase me as I ran around our home. At night I would beg Mama to let them sleep in my bed.

"They are not potty-trained yet," she would say.

The only time my mother allowed the puppies to sleep with us was when we slept in the salon. They would start howling really loud, even before any of us could hear the shelling.

"Baba, why are Lulu and Murjan making weird sounds?" I asked.

"Dogs don't like loud noises. That's why."

"I don't either. It hurts my ears."

My parents got into the habit of placing mattresses on the salon's floor as soon as the sun departed our city. The minute the shelling started, they would rush into our bedroom and carry my sister and me to the salon. When the bombardment got closer and louder, Mama would hug Arwa and Baba would hug me. He would wrap his arms around me, trying to shield me from harm. Although his embrace was so tight, almost suffocating, he made me feel safe, even when the shelling got so loud, piercing my ears.

After one night of particularly heavy shelling, I heard my mother tell my father, "Tomorrow I'm going to call my cousin Abdo and ask him to take the girls to Damascus."

"Good idea. The fighting is getting worse. They shouldn't experience this."

"Amo Abdo is coming tomorrow to take you and Arwa to Damascus. Aunt Nahida is waiting for you. She bought you lots of toys," my mother said, while packing clothes into two small suitcases she had placed on Arwa's bed.

"Will you come with us, Mama?" I asked.

"No *habibti*, sweetheart, I can't. I have to stay with your baba."

"But I don't want to go. I want to stay with you."

"Your baba and I will be coming soon," Mama said.

When Amo Abdo appeared at our door the next morning, I was terrified.

"I don't like you. I am not going with you," I said as I ran into my room.

"Anan, you should not say this to Amo Abdo. It is *eib*, shameful," said my mother.

"But I want to stay with you."

"I will come to Damascus soon. Come say sorry to Amo Abdo and have some breakfast."

"I'm not hungry."

My mother carried me to the dining-room table where Amo Abdo was sitting with Arwa. My father had already gone to work. After having a quick breakfast, Amo Abdo got up, grabbed our two suitcases and said, "It's time. We have a long way to go."

Mama followed him. She walked my sister Arwa and me to his big car, holding our hands.

"Be good, now. Don't give Amo Abdo a hard time."

I wrapped my arms around my mother's thigh really hard and began to cry.

"Please Mama, I don't want to go. I want to stay with you."

With teary eyes she said, "Your father and I will come very soon. I promise."

"Can I take Lulu and Murjan with me?"

"No *habibti*, you can't," said my mother. She scooped me off the sidewalk and carried me to the backseat of Amo Abdo's car. Then she bent over to kiss me.

"Why are you crying, Mama?"

She patted my head, then she said, "Abdo, wait a minute. I forgot their toys."

Mama ran into the house and came back with my favorite doll, some other toys and some books. She also brought food and two thermoses, one with milk and one with coffee.

"I don't want to go. I want my Lulu and Murjan," I screamed as Amo Abdo started to drive. Mama stood there. From the large backseat window, I watched her get smaller and smaller. Then she totally disappeared.

Amo Abdo was not the most child-friendly uncle. I was only three and a half years old at the time, but I have a vivid memory of our trip to Damascus. I cried my heart out.

"I said stop crying," Amo Abdo would yell, which made me wail.

"Arwa, talk to your sister. Make her stop crying."

The more he yelled, the louder I cried. Arwa, acting like the big sister, tried her best to comfort me. She would hold me and say, "Don't cry Anan. We will be at Beit Jido soon. Khalto Suad and Khalto Nahida are waiting for us." Or she would try to distract me, "Here's your favorite doll, look how beautiful it is. Look what Mama put in your bag—chocolate and cookies. You want some?"

"No, no," I cried back. "I want my mama." Then I pleaded with Amo Abdo, "I do love you, Amo Abdo. Please take me back to my mama."

Exhausted, I finally I fell asleep.

In the Old City of Damascus, I sat on the doorstep of my grandfather's very large and very old house, waiting for Mama and Baba.[5] I sat there separated from my parents and separating myself from my relatives living in this house. I sat on the street side of a long, dark, L-shaped corridor that led to a bright and sunny courtyard with colorful tiles, *kabbad* and *narinje* citrus fruit trees, a jasmine tree, and lots of flowerpots and a big fountain.

Jido's house was much bigger than our home in Jerusalem. I slept in the *kaser,* a sleeping quarter on the third floor, with my Aunt Nahida and cousin Aida, while Arwa slept with Aunt Suad on the other side of the house. The stone stairways leading to the bedrooms were steep and dark. At night, I was scared to go to bed alone, or even to the kitchen, which was on the same level of the courtyard where my aunts spent their evenings.

"There is nothing to be scared of," my Aunt Suad would say.

"But what if I get lost?"

"No one ever got lost here. You're a big girl. You can go to bed by yourself."

"I'll take her," Arwa said as she held my hand and walked me to my bed.

When my parents sent my sister Arwa and me to Jido's, they promised they would come soon to get us. Every morning, I would take my favorite spot at the doorstep looking toward the end of Sawaf Street, so narrow no car could get through. I would look for a car to stop and for my parents to get out. Each car brought excitement, hope and disappointment. Some days I would quietly cry. Other days I would go inside, angry with my parents, only to come back out a few minutes later, hoping that this time they would come.

Aunt Nahida must have herself been worried about my parents and other relatives. She was also aware of my anxiety and how much I missed my parents. Often she would come to the doorstep saying, "Anan, it's getting cold. Come inside. You can't sit at the doorstep all day long."

"I want to wait for Mama and Baba."

"When they come, they'll ring the doorbell."

"But what if they never come back?"

"Stop worrying. Of course they will come."

Most days, I refused to come in. Arwa would sit with me or ask me to come inside and play with her.

"I don't want to play. You go play with Aida."

"Aida is too young. She doesn't know how to play."

Sometimes, Aunt Nahida would bring Aida, who was a year younger than me, to keep me company.

"Keep an eye on Aida, and you two stay here. Do not go into the street."

Sitting there doing nothing, Aida would get bored and go inside. My aunt often came to the doorstep bringing me something to eat or drink: a piece of fruit, a sandwich, a glass of milk or freshly squeezed tomato juice. She would gently try to get me inside the house, promising me that my parents would come soon.

"When?"

"Soon," she would say, then quickly add, "*Inshallah*, God willing."

We stayed in Damascus for almost a full year. I will never forget my fear that I might never see Mama and Baba again, or how much I yearned for our puppies Lulu and Murjan.

Aunt Nahida did all she could to comfort me. When I got too anxious, sad or angry, I would retreat to one of the rooms, refusing to talk to anyone. Aunt Nahida would put me in her warm lap and sing some lullaby until I fell asleep. Every day she promised me that my parents would be coming soon.

Soon, it was not. It was way too long for me to be separated from my parents and my two puppies—my most vivid and pleasant memories of Palestine.

When my parents finally came, I ran into the small room by the courtyard and closed the door.

"Leave me alone. I don't want to talk to you," I told my mother when she came to the door.

"Open the door Anan. I missed you. Come give Mama a big hug and a kiss."

"No. You lied to me. You said you'd come soon."

I wasn't the only one who cried. My aunts did, too. Even Jido cried. I wondered if they were as mad at my parents as I was, for not coming any sooner.

When the news spread about my parents' arrival, my grandfather's house filled with aunts, uncles, cousins, neighbors and friends—many of whom I'd never seen before. They kept saying "*Nushkur Allah,* thank God…we were so worried about you. Don't worry, you will go back to your home soon…God is generous, *Allah kareem."*

My parents stayed at my jido's home for about a week. The night before we were to leave, the same bunch of people came back. All of the women, including my mother and aunts, started to cry again as they said their goodbyes. I cried too, although I didn't understand why everyone was crying.

"Go to bed now," my mama said. "Tomorrow we have to leave early."

"I'm not going with you. I want to stay with Aunt Nahida," I objected, still mad at my parents.

When Khalto Nahida hugged me early that morning, saying, "I'm going to miss you, Anan," I didn't want to let go of her, dreading a new separation and renewed longing.

"Khalto Nahida, I want to stay with you," I begged.

"Habibti, you have been waiting for your parents for so long. You should be happy to go with them."

"Can you come with us…please?"

"I can't. I have to go to work. But I promise you I'll bring Aida and come to visit you soon."

Reluctantly, I let go of her and went to hold my father's hand. I was confused. I didn't know if I wanted to stay with my aunt or go with my parents.

"Be careful…*Allah ma'akum…Allah yehmeekum,* may God be with you and protect you," chanted my aunts, as we gathered our few belongings and crammed ourselves into my father's small car.

My father, who was driving, was lost in his own thoughts, and so was my mother. Their deadly silence frightened me. I could only hear the tires spinning against the road. I would be quiet for a while, staring out the window or looking in the mirror at my parents' gloomy faces. But, being kids, Arwa and I soon started playing, arguing and asking questions.

"Be quiet. Your father isn't feeling well," Mama kept telling us.

"What's wrong, Baba? Why are you not feeling well?" I asked.

"I'm fine habibti, I am fine."

My father didn't say much until we were near the end of our trip. He tried to explain to my sister and me that although we were going home, it wouldn't be to the same house we had lived in before.

"What do you mean, Baba? Aren't we going home?" Arwa asked.

"Of course we are, but our new home is in a different neighborhood of Jerusalem. We'll have neighbors with young children you can play with."

"What about our neighbor's kids, Abla and Ahmed? Will they be there?" Arwa asked.

"And what about Lulu and Murjan?" I asked anxiously.

"No. Lulu and Murjan are not going to be there."

"Why not? Where are they? What happened to them?"

"We had to leave them behind," said my father.

"How could you leave them? I want my puppies."

"I promise I will get you new ones as soon as we are settled."

"But I don't want new ones. I want my Lulu and Murjan."

My father tried to explain to me why they had had to leave the puppies behind as he and my mother fled for their lives. Although my father was once a teacher, like my Aunt Nahida, he couldn't make me, at the age of four, understand.

I am now seventy years old. I still cannot understand how what happened in 1948 could actually happen.

Me at age two in West Jerusalem, 1947.

3. It's a Boy, It's a Boy—Thank God It's a Boy!

Damascus, 1949

Only a few months after we settled into our new home in East Jerusalem, Baba drove my mother, Arwa and me to our jido's home in Damascus. Mama was in her last month of pregnancy. As was the tradition of her time, she went to her family's home to deliver the baby.

Two days after we arrived at Beit Jido, I woke up to find my father already fully dressed in his dark suit, a white shirt and striped red tie. He was with my mother and aunts in the courtyard, and they were drinking their morning coffee. Arwa was sitting next to him. Also beside him was his *tarbush*, his red fez hat.

"Where are you going, Baba?" I asked.

"He is going back to Jerusalem," Arwa answered for him.

"Are you going alone? How about us?"

"I have to go back to work. You stay here with your mother and sister."

My father was still working at the Huna al-Quds radio station, which reopened after 1948 in Ramallah, only eight miles from our home in East Jerusalem.

I pushed his tarbush aside and sat next to him. When he hugged me to say goodbye, I started to cry.

"Please Baba, don't go."

"Habibti, don't be upset. I will be back soon."

"You said this before, but you were gone for a long, long time."

"This time it won't be long. I promise. I'll come back as soon as the baby is born."

"Why are you crying?" said Arwa. "He'll be back. You're such a crybaby."

"Be nice to your sister. Don't say that to her," said Baba.

"I am nice to her, but she cries a lot."

Baba was big on telling the truth. But it was hard for me to believe him when he told me he would be back soon. I was terrified that he might be gone for a long time, just like he and Mama had before. Having our mother with us was a bit comforting, although she hardly paid us much attention, especially when we were at Beit Jido.

A few days after Baba left, I woke up with a start. So much noise and excitement was coming from the courtyard. It was still early, but the oppressive August sun was already blazing. Aunt Fariza was ululating, "It's a boy, it's a boy—thank God, it's a boy!"

Slowly I descended the steep stairway to the courtyard, drawn by all the commotion. My three aunts were sitting on the *diwan* in the courtyard, along with the midwife, Sabrieh Khanum. Khalto Fariza, who had been staying at Beit Jido in anticipation of my mother delivering the baby, was still in her nightgown, as were my other aunts, Suad and Nahida. I don't know when Sabrieh Khanum came over. My aunts must have called her in the middle of the night when my mother was ready to deliver.

When Aunt Fariza, who was married but didn't have any children, saw me, she hugged me and said, "Congratulations, *mabrook!* You should be very happy. You have a brother now."

I ran upstairs to wake my sister.

"Arwa, Arwa, wake up! Mama had a baby boy."

"You're lying to me."

"No. Wallah, I swear, it's a boy."

"Really?"

Reluctantly Arwa got up, and she and I went downstairs to where my aunts were gathering. When Khalto Fariza saw Arwa, she said the same thing, "*Mabrook*, congratulations. You should be very happy. You have a brother now." Tears ran down her cheeks.

"Khalto, why are you crying?" I asked.

"These are happy tears. I am so happy you have a brother. He will carry your father's name."

"I have my father's name, and he has my name, too. He is Abu

Arwa," said my sister, acting proud and cocky.

"I have his name, too," I said, then ran with Arwa to the lower qa'ah to see Mama and our new brother.

"Leave your mother alone. She and the baby need some rest," said Khalto Suad, as we tried to enter the room.

"But I want to see my baby brother," I protested.

"They are both asleep now. Wait until they wake up. Let's call your father."

"Thank God she had a boy," said Aunt Fariza again. "Can you imagine calling to tell him he has a third girl?"

Arwa and I followed my aunt to a small room where the phone was. After she placed a call with the operator, we sat there waiting.

"Khalto, can I talk to Baba?" I asked.

"I want to talk him too," said Arwa.

"Inshallah."

Tired of waiting, we left the room and went to the kitchen to join cousin Aida and Aunt Nahida. By the time we came back, Khalto Suad had already talked to my father.

"Is Baba coming?" I asked.

"Of course. He is coming to see the baby."

"When is he coming? How long he is staying?" asked Khalto Fariza.

"He told me he is taking a few days of vacation starting the day after tomorrow. He should be here by Thursday afternoon."

In less than an hour, Khalto Isa'af came with her two daughters, Nabila and Maysa. By noon, large trays of baklava and other sweets were delivered from Ghrawi sweet shop. By late afternoon Beit Jido was packed with women coming to congratulate my mother, bringing her and the baby all kinds of gifts. They sat with my aunts, drinking fresh lemonade and eating sweets and *karawyeh,* a special caraway pudding served when a baby is born. For the first three days, Mama stayed mostly in her room with Ayman. Then she started to join the visitors. And every single woman would tell her, "Mabrook, congratulations! Thank God you have a boy."

Before my mom could show Ayman to the guests, Aunt Fariza went to Souq al-Hamadyeh and bought a small golden pendant engraved with a verse from the Quran and a blue bead to protect Ayman from evil eyes.

"Here Siham, pin these to Ayman's clothes."

My mother did not believe in these myths, but she would keep these pinned to Ayman's clothes for a couple of years, just in case her sister was right.

Although I was not yet five years old at the time, I still remember all the pride and joy associated with my brother's birth. Everyone kept telling me over and over again that I should be very happy to have a brother. But I never recall being told that I was lucky to have a sister. It was at that very early age that I came to realize that boys are more precious than girls. That made me so mad that I secretly wished Mama had had another girl.

One afternoon, while my mother was napping, Arwa said, "Let's go see how Ayman is really different."

We tiptoed into the room where Ayman was sleeping peacefully, trying not to wake up my mother who was napping in the adjacent room. Quietly, Arwa and I undressed Ayman and sat there staring at his genitals. When I touched his penis he started to cry.

"Why did you do that?" said Arwa as we clumsily tried to put his diaper back on. But he started to cry even louder.

"What the hell are you doing in here?" my mother yelled at us as she entered the room.

"We just wanted to see what he looks like," said Arwa.

"Leave your brother alone, and don't you ever do that again."

We ran down the stairway giggling. "He looks weird," Arwa said. "I am glad I don't have that thing coming out of me."

"He doesn't look like Baba," I said. "Does he?"

"No, he doesn't," said Arwa.

Sure enough, my father arrived two days after Ayman was born, and my uncles came to congratulate him. And when Uncle Rashad told my father, "Now we can call you Abu Ayman," Father responded, "I am, and will always be, Abu Arwa. She is the one who made me a father."

My father stayed for only a couple of days. Then he was ready to leave again.

"Baba, why do you keep leaving us? Can't you stay?"

"Habibti, I have to go back to work. I will be back in a month. Then we can all go home together."

"Why do you get upset every time Baba leaves?" asked Arwa.

"What if he never comes back?"

"You're silly. He always comes back."

Sure enough, my father came home after my mother had concluded her forty days of being taken care of by her family. That was another observed tradition: women stayed at their family's home for forty days after giving birth, the time believed to be needed for a woman to regain her strength.

With our new family addition, we said farewell to my aunts and uncles, and drove the one hundred forty miles to our home in East Jerusalem. With us came boxes and boxes of Ghrawi sweets in anticipation of the congratulating guests. Before we had time to settle in, all of our neighbors and friends came to my parents' home to congratulate them on having a boy and commented on how healthy and beautiful Ayman was. As if it was not enough to have a super-hyper sister who was more beautiful, outgoing and funny than I was, now I had a brother who drew even more admiration from whomever laid an eye on him, saying, "*Ismallah*, in the name of God, he is so gorgeous!" Truth be told, Ayman was a very attractive child. He was also very smart and charming, and before long he developed a great sense of humor.

~

Our stay in East Jerusalem did not last long. Ayman was hardly a year old when we had to pack our belongings, say our goodbyes again and move to Amman where my father had landed a new job. By then I was attached to our neighbor, Amo Adli, and his beautiful and colorful birds. I didn't want to leave. I especially liked the tiny yellow canaries that sang a lot, and the large red and green parrot whom Amo Adli taught to say my name.

Shortly after we moved from Jerusalem to Amman, my father packed us up again in his small car and took us back to Damascus. My mother was pregnant with her fourth and last child. As was the case with Ayman's birth, my father drove us to Beit Jido, stayed for a couple of days, then went back to Jerusalem. Soon, on a beautiful April morning, my sister Suad was born. We nicknamed her Susu.

On the day of her birth, midwife Sabrieh Khanum and my two married aunts, Fariza and Isa'af, arrived early at Beit Jido. My four aunts seemed to be running back and forth, up the stairway to where my mother was and back down to the kitchen, totally unclear about what they were doing.

"Arwa, is Mama going to have her baby today?" I asked.

"I think so. That's why our aunts and Sabrieh Khanum are all here."

"Come here, Arwa," called Aunt Suad, "Listen to me carefully. I want you to take your sister and go to *al-kaser*. Take your toys and books with you."

"I don't want to go with Anan. She's no fun. She doesn't like to play."

"That's not true. I like to play, but you always win."

"Don't start now," Khalto Suad said. "Just go upstairs. Don't let me hear you fighting or arguing. And don't come back until I call you. You understand?"

"Yes Khalto, we do," we said in unison.

Al-kaser was the part of the house farthest from the *franka,* the room on the second floor, where my mother was about to deliver her baby. It had two adjacent bedrooms and large windows overlooking the courtyard. We waited, we played and we argued, but mostly we sat on the wide windowsills, watching the courtyard. After what felt like forever, Aunt Nahida sent the new housekeeper, Fawziyeh, to get us.

"Your aunts said you can come down now. Your mother had another girl. What a pity."

We walked down the stairway in anticipation. The excitement that accompanied Ayman's birth was not there. None of my aunts seemed happy. Arwa ran toward the franka where my mother was, asking, "Is Mama okay?"

"Of course she is," said Khalto Suad.

"How about the baby?"

"The baby is fine. You have another sister," said Aunt Fariza, clearly disappointed.

"Khalto Suad, how come you love boys more?" Arwa asked.

"Who said we do?"

"You don't seem to be happy, like when Ayman was born."

"Ya Arwa ya habibti, sweetheart, I will never ever love a child—boy or girl—more than I love you. You know that, don't you?

"I do…I do."

Arwa was my Aunt Suad's favorite. But I was not as convinced that she, or any of my other aunts, were happy that my mother had a girl. When my cousin Aida came home from school, I ran to open the door. I wanted to be the one to tell her the news.

"Mama had a baby girl. I don't think my aunts are happy."

In the late afternoon, we were allowed to see Mama and the baby.

"What's her name?" I asked.

"Suad. I want to name her after my sister."

"Mama, are you upset because you had a girl?" asked Arwa.

"Of course not. *Mafi mettel elbanat*, there is nothing like girls. I love you and Anan very much. Come give me a kiss."

"Don't lie now," said Aunt Suad, "You wanted a boy, didn't you?"

"You're right, I did. But only because I wanted Ayman to have a brother."

By noon, sweet trays were delivered, karawyeh was prepared and women guests arrived to congratulate my mother, bringing their gifts to her and the baby. However, the mood was not as celebratory as when Ayman was born.

My father came back from Jerusalem to see the baby. Then he was gone. He came back a month or so later to take us home. Again Arwa asked, "Baba are you upset Mama had a girl?"

"Of course not," said my father. Then he hugged Arwa and said, "You should never, ever think I'd rather have a boy."

As it turned out, Suad was not only the apple of my father's eye, but mine too. I loved her and took care of her, first as if she was my toy, and later, as if she were my own daughter.

"You claimed Susu to be yours the day she was born," my mother used to say.

Although I was only six and a half years older than Suad, I was very attached to and protective of her, probably out of jealousy of Ayman, who got so much attention from family, neighbors and friends. Not only was he the boy, he was also stunningly beautiful.

4. My Lamb

East Jerusalem, 1949[6]

The bright sun invaded my bedroom, telling me it was time to get up. I stared at the intricate design on the walls, as the light seeped through the lace curtains. I was mesmerized by the soft movements of the patterns elicited by the morning breeze flirting with the curtains. Slowly, I got out of my bed and walked to my bedroom balcony. The sun was so bright that I had a hard time keeping my eyes open.

The morning air was warm and fresh. A deep green grass, dotted with red and yellow flowers, covered the hillside next to our home. It was spring, a season when shepherds brought their herds of sheep and goats to graze. I stood at the balcony soaking up the sun and watching the world come to life. Suddenly I spotted a shiny, pitch-black baby goat emerging from its mother. The shepherd sat next to the mother, comforting her. I knew something exciting was happening, but I was not sure what.

"Arwa! Mama!" I screamed.

Arwa, with whom I shared a bedroom, shifted in her bed, covered her head with the sheet and rolled over to face the wall. Unable to contain my excitement, I started jumping and yelling.

"Mama come, please come now!"

Hurriedly she came, expecting the worst.

"What is it? Why are you screaming?"

"Look Mama, look," I said, pointing.

Arwa, who hadn't been able to fall back to sleep, got excited and jumped out of her bed saying, "What is it? What are you looking at?"

Together, Mama, Arwa and I stood there watching the baby goat gradually emerge. We watched until the newborn was able to stand on its own feet.

"Can I have a baby lamb?" I asked my mother.

"I thought you wanted puppies like Lulu and Murjan."

"I changed my mind. I want a baby lamb."

"That is a baby goat."

Not knowing the difference, I insisted that what I wanted was a baby lamb. A few weeks later, my father came home holding something in his arms.

"Anan, Anan, look what I've got for you!"

A mischievous smile stretched across his face as he put the four-legged creature next to me.

I looked at the small creature and took a step back. The lamb took a step toward me. I took another step backward, and it took another step forward. I ran to my room, the lamb followed me. I jumped on my bed begging my father, "Please Baba, take it away. It's scared of me. God will punish me if I scare it any more."

That was my father's favorite story about my childhood.

As much as I wanted a baby lamb, once I got it, I didn't like it at all. It frightened me. Once in a while I would muster my courage and decide to take it to graze on the hill by our home, like a shepherd.

"You can't take it there, it will run away. Its food is in the backyard," Mama would say.

"Can you put it on a leash?"

"It's not a dog. You can't put a lamb on a leash," Arwa said.

"Yes I can. Mama will help me."

"Remember how we killed our chicken when we put it in a bag because we were afraid it would run? If you put the lamb on a leash, it'll choke and die."

"No it won't."

After my tireless pleading, my mother tied a long rope around the poor lamb's neck. I held the rope while trying to keep as much distance between us as I could. The minute the lamb came close to me, I let it loose and ran inside the house.

My parents and sister tried their best to demonstrate how

harmless that lamb was, but I was not about to be convinced.

"Look, it's not going to hurt you," Arwa would say, placing her hand on its mouth.

"I don't like it. I want birds like Amo Adli's."

~

In our East Jerusalem home, in the Sheikh Jarrah neighborhood where we moved after 1948, we lived in the middle flat of a three-story home. Amo Adli lived in the flat above us with his widowed mother and younger brother. Their flat had a large veranda where he kept different kinds of birds. He had small yellow canaries that sang all day until his mother, Khalto Um Adli, got tired of the noise and covered their cages with dark cloths. The parrots were larger and more colorful, with red, yellow and green feathers. They could actually say a few words.

Whenever I saw Amo Adli coming home, I would run toward him saying, "Amo Adli, can I come upstairs with you? Can I help you feed the birds?"

"Of course you can."

He would lift me up onto his shoulders and off we'd go to his house.

After kissing his mother's forehead, he would reach to the shelf where he kept their food.

"Here you go," he would say, as he put some birdseed in my tiny hands.

One morning, the day before Eid al-Adha, the Muslim holiday, my mother told Arwa and me, "Why don't you take your cousin Aida and show her our neighborhood?" Aida had come from Damascus with her mother, Aunt Nahida, to spend the eid with us.

"Can I take her upstairs to see Amo Adli's birds?" I asked.

"I want to see the birds," said Aida excitedly.

"Not today," said Mama. "Amo Adli is not home. You can go there later."

"But *Khalto Um Adli*[7] is upstairs," I told my mother.

"She doesn't want to be bothered. You go with Arwa and show Aida your new school. Go visit your friend Hanan, go buy some candies," said my mother.

"I want ice cream," said Arwa. "Please Mama, can I buy some?"

"Yes you can."

The list of things my mother told us we could do was quite long, and the spending money was more than we ever had. Arwa and I loved playing tour guides in our Jerusalem neighborhood. We were on our own familiar terrain, proud to be the expert hosts.

"Your mama lets you go to all these places by yourself?" asked Aida.

"Not really. She wants us to show you around." Arwa said.

"But there's not much to see."

Aida was getting antsy. She wanted to go back home.

"Let me show you my school. It's just around the corner," Arwa said. "Then we can go get ice cream."

A few minutes later we got to the neighborhood ice-cream store.

"This place doesn't have much, not like Bakdash," said Aida, referring to the historic ice-cream parlor in Damascus.

"You sound like Mama," I said. "'Everything is better in Damascus.'"

The next morning, there was no trace of my lamb. I ran to my mother.

"Mama, the lamb is gone."

"I know. I'm sorry. It ran away."

"It's okay, Mama. Can I have a puppy now? Or can I have birds like the ones at Amo Adli's?"

"Inshallah," my mother said.

I don't remember being saddened by the lamb's disappearance. I never missed it or even thought about it beyond that day. A few months after the lamb vanished, my mother told my sister Arwa and me, "Your father got a new good job. Once the school year is over, we will be moving to Amman."

"I don't want to leave my school. I don't want to leave Amo Adli and the birds."

"Amman is not far. We can visit on weekends. Amo Adli will also visit us. We're going to have a big house with a nice garden. You can get a puppy there."

"But I don't want to go."

Washington, DC, 1994

The night was unusually cold, with a blizzard shutting down most of the city. My friend and I took refuge in a neighborhood bar, where two drinks for the price of one were still served at happy hour. Light-headed from the first round, I started chatting away, reminiscing about my childhood, about Jerusalem and about my lamb. To my surprise, I said matter-of-factly, "My parents asked me to take my cousin Aida on a neighborhood tour and while I was gone they slaughtered my lamb for the Eid al-Adha feast."

"You mean they ate your pet?" asked my friend.

"Yes. They did. Somehow I knew what had really happened, but I didn't think or say anything about it all these years, nor did my parents." Then I added, "How could they do that to me? That was really cruel."

To my surprise, tears were pouring down my face. I was crying, despite myself. It felt so awkward shedding all those tears forty-five years later over a lamb I was relieved to have disappeared. I was taken by the intensity of my emotions. Was I really crying over the loss of my lamb, I wondered? Or was it the loss of my father, the loss of my home, and the loss of my Jerusalem? Or was I crying over the sacrifice of my lamb to save the son(s) of Abraham?[8]

5. FAMILY REUNIONS

East Jerusalem, 1950

Startled, I sat up in bed rubbing my eyes, chasing away the bad dream and its loud voices. But was it a dream, or were these voices real?

"Arwa. Arwa, wake up," I begged.

"Leave me alone. I want to sleep."

"Arwa, please get up. I think there are men in our house."

"No one is here. Go back to sleep."

"I'm scared. Can't you hear them?"

"Go tell Baba and Mama," Arwa said, turning her back to me, drifting away.

Not getting much sympathy from my sister, who loved to sleep, I got out of bed, put on my slippers and warily walked to my parents' room. Only my mother was there.

"Mama, I hear men in the house."

"Be quiet. Don't wake up Ayman."

Ayman was sleeping in a small room adjacent to my parents' room.

"Where is Baba?"

"He's in the living room."

"Who's here?"

"I don't know. I want to sleep. Your father is there, you can go find out."

"Can you come with me? I don't want to go by myself."

"You're going to be six years old soon. Just go."

To my surprise, my father was in the living room with a stranger. He was still in his pajamas, a big no-no for my father. He never let anyone but Mama and us kids see him in his pajamas. The strange man resembled my father but was much darker. They were sitting on the sofa, close to each other, seemingly very content. They kept repeating themselves.

"Finally…Nushkur Allah."

"I've missed you."

"I was worried I might never find you."

"Where have you been?"

Hesitant to come in but too curious to leave, I stood by the door watching. I wanted to know who this stranger was knocking at our door in the dark.

"Good morning, Anan," said my father. "Come say hello to your amo. This is my brother Omar. Remember, I told you about him?"[9]

"Come here. Come give Amo a hug," said the stranger with a big smile on his face.

Not wanting to get close, I just stood there, staring.

"Anan, come say hello to your amo," my father said again, his voice stern.

Not daring to defy him, I slowly walked toward our guest. Before reaching him, he stretched his arms out and grabbed me. He sat me on his lap, embraced me really hard and kept kissing my face and head. I wanted to get away from him. He looked poor and dirty. His clothes had big stains, he smelled like rotten food and his kisses were slimy.

"Nushkur Allah, I found you. I'm so happy to see you. You've grown so much."

With his thumb, he pressed the corner of his eye, wiping away a tear.

"Omar, you must be tired. Let me show you the bathroom. You go wash up and I will get you some clean clothes," my father said. Then he turned to me. "Go back to your bed. Let Amo get some sleep."

Although I was told this strange man was my uncle, I didn't remember ever seeing him, or any of my father's relatives, before.

"Baba, how come I never saw Amo before?" I asked.

"You did. Probably you don't remember."

"Is he your real brother? Where was he? How come he keeps saying 'Nushkur Allah, I found you?'"

"Because we lost each other after the *Nakba*.[10] You don't have to worry about that. He is with us now."

I don't know how my uncle found us or where he was, but I do remember his contagious laugh.

"Come here Anan, come and sit in my lap" or "Come and give Amo Omar a hug," he often said. Whenever we were in the same room, he would grab Arwa or me and put us on his lap, or we'd sit on his back as he crawled on the floor playing horsey. Unlike my father, Amo Omar was not that serious. He laughed a lot and loved to trick my sister and me.

One morning Amo Omar took a long bath and got all dressed up in a dark suit, a white shirt, a tie and shiny black shoes. He looked like my father. He even had a red tarbush with him that rested on top of his new, brown leather suitcase. I had never seen Amo Omar dressed like that before, or wearing a tarbush.

"Where you going, Amo?" I asked.

"I'm going to Amman and maybe later to Kuwait."

"Will you come back soon?"

"No habibti. Where I am going is far. But inshallah, it won't be long before I see you again.

"Why do you have to go so far? I'll miss you."

"I'll miss you too. But I need to find a job, and not many are available around here."

A dark sorrow took hold of me. I cried when Amo left. I cried again in my bed the night he was gone, wondering why everyone had to leave and who would be leaving me next.

Amman, 1953

Since we'd moved there in 1951, my father had been talking about wanting to bring his sister Naima to live in Amman. I had never met my aunt, but Baba said she was living in a refugee camp in Gaza.

"Now that we and Omar are settled in Amman, I need to bring my sister Naima and her family to live here as well."

"We're not moving anymore?" I asked my father. I was nine years old, had made a few friends and liked my school and teachers. The thought of moving again was terrifying.

"I hope not. That's why I want to bring my sister and her family here. I can't leave them in a refugee camp any longer."

"Baba, why does your sister live in a refugee camp? How far is Gaza? Can we go visit her?"

"It's not that easy to visit," my father explained.

"Why not?"

"You're too young to understand. One day I'll tell you all about it. For now let's just hope I can bring her."

I used to get really mad when my father would tell me I was too young to understand. All he and his friends talked about was the war, the Nakba, their lost homes and shattered families. Some of his friends even cried when they shared their sorrows. But whenever I asked him to tell me more, he would say that I was too young, or he would change the subject.

"Why don't you tell me about your school?" he would say. "Tell me about the last story you read."

My father got me many books. Unlike the stories he and his friends shared, the stories in my books always had happy endings.

On a bright but not too hot summer day, my father came home from work early and announced the safe arrival of his sister and her family.

"Finally, they arrived. They're at Khaled's house."

Khaled was my aunt's older stepson.[11]

"How are they?" asked my mother.

"Tired. They traveled from Gaza to Cairo by car, then took a plane from Cairo. It's a hard, long trip, especially with six children."

"Did Rihab come with them?" asked my mother.

Rihab, Khaled's sister and my aunt's stepdaughter, was a few years older than the rest of her children.

"Yes, she did. Otherwise it would have been harder for Naima and her husband to handle all the kids and luggage, though they didn't have much." Then my father added, "I'm going back this afternoon. I want you to come with me."

"Inshallah," said my mother. By then I was old enough to understand that my mother would rather invoke the name of Allah than say no.

Khaled's small living room was packed. Younger kids sat on adults' laps. Older ones were asked to sit on the floor to make room for my father, my sister Arwa and me. After exchanging a few hellos, my father said, "This is Arwa and this is Anan. Siham will come soon to welcome you." Then he told Arwa and me, "This is my sister Naima I have been telling you about. This is Amo Mahmoud, her husband, and these are their children."

"Oh my God. You've grown so much. Look at you. You are so beautiful," said Aunt Naima as she hugged us while blowing her nose and wiping her tears with a large white handkerchief. "These are your cousins," she said, pointing as she recited each name: "Rihab, Hani, Marwan, Nihal, Mohammad, Suzan and baby Osama."

I looked at them, one at a time. So many. *How was I supposed to remember all their names?* My aunt kept pulling the wrinkled handkerchief out of her sleeve to wipe tears that ran past the puffy, dark circles under her eyes. My father kept telling her, "Naima, stop crying. Don't worry. Everything is going to be alright."

"Baba, why was Aunt Naima crying?" I asked as we were driving home.

"She was just tired from traveling."

"Why were they living in Gaza?"

"I will tell you about it later."

When I asked Aunt Naima why she was living in Gaza, she said, "Gaza was not that far from Jaffa, where we lived before the war. For the first couple of years, we kept hoping to go back home."

"Will you go back?" I asked.

"Allah kareem, I hate to give up. But as time passed, I decided to move to Amman where your father and my brother Omar live. Alhamdulillah, your father was able to find us and help us move here. I want my kids to get a good education."

"My baba wants us to get a good education, too. He said it is the one thing no one can take away from us."

"Your baba is right. Education is our salvation."[12] I didn't understand what that meant, but there were many things about my father's family I didn't understand then.

My father, with his younger brother, my Uncle Omar, in Jaffa around 1926.

6. Damascus Nights

Damascus, 1955

We emerged from the various parts of my grandfather's house and gathered in the courtyard. The day was still bright, but the sun had softened, allowing a gentle breeze to cool the place. The aroma of Turkish coffee, mixed with cardamom, filled the air—a sign that my two aunts, with whom we spent most of our summers, were up from their nap.

My jido's house was large and grand; twenty-eight rooms occupied three floors. The large courtyard, with its colorful tiles, flowing fountain, cooing pigeons and scented flowers made the place feel magical. One couldn't help but be mesmerized by the sounds and smells this home had to offer.

This elegant house told a story of money and power, as well as a story of the end of an era. It was built for an extended family with aunts, uncles and lots of children, but I only remember my jido, my two aunts—Suad and Nahida—who never got married, and my cousin Aida, my Aunt Nahida's adopted daughter, living there. My maternal grandmother died when I was only two years old, and sadly I have no memory

Plaque at Beit Jabri, the house of my mother's family—in this story, Beit Jido, Grandfather's House—built in 1737.

of her. On the other hand, my grandfather died when I was fourteen, and he was the only grandparent I got to know and love.

My jido was born in this house, and so were all his children and some of his grandchildren, including my three siblings and me. Many of us were delivered by the neighborhood midwife, Sabrieh Khanum, who claimed to have also delivered my mother. Those of us who were born in the summertime, including Arwa and Ayman, came into this life in the lower qa'ah, the large hall on the first floor. Those who were born in the wintertime, like Susu and myself, were delivered in the franka on the second floor.

Aunt Nahida was a teacher. She loved kids and took the time to explain things to us. When I asked her why they lived in such a large house, she said, "In the old days those born in this house stayed, even after they got married and had their own children."

"How come they don't live here anymore?" I asked.

"Because they became modern and didn't want to live with others. They wanted to be on their own."

I didn't know if that was good or bad, but I figured my parents must have been modern because we lived on our own.

**My mother's Jabri family, in Damascus, around 1937.
My mother is second from the right.**

Many of the rooms in my jido's home had funny names, like *abo*, *qa'ah*, *liwan*, *salon*, *muraba'a* and *franka*. With such a big house, it was easier to give the rooms names so we knew which room someone was talking about. The *diar*, a beautiful courtyard, was the center of the house, where my aunts and their guests spent most of their day, except for their afternoon nap. Before lunch they drank lots of Turkish coffee and fresh lemonade, and sewed and embroidered dresses for their nieces. Most days a neighbor, a friend or one of my two married aunts—Isa'af and Fariza—would stop by.

In the evenings, my aunts spent their time playing cards and Parcheesi,[13] while enjoying the scent of jasmine and gardenia as it became stronger in the late hours of the night. They ate lots of watermelon, which they put in the courtyard fountain for a few hours to chill. When Jido came home from work, he also ate watermelon and played cards with my aunts. Jido played cards with me, too. He let me win and gave me a new silver coin for winning. Jido always had shiny coins.

My jido's house was on Zqaq al-Sawwaf, or Sawwaf Alley, in the Old City. The outside neighborhood was as fascinating as the inside of the house. At one end of the narrow street, where cars could not pass through, was Ras el Hara, a small square with a fountain of fresh spring water, including a small section for animals—mostly donkeys and horses. There was also a small grocery store and a candy-and-slush store featuring crushed ices in an assortment of syrupy flavors. My favorite was the baker. I loved it when my aunts asked me to go get some fresh bread. Hot and crunchy, I had a hard time not eating some on my way home. I also loved watching the shepherd and his goats stopping at houses in the neighborhood. We would bring our own pot and get milk from the goat, then boil it well before drinking it.

From the square, three streets led to other neighborhoods. But the most exciting part was on the other side of Zqaq al-Sawwaf, the endless maze of alley streets. One would take you to the Umayyad Mosque and the historic al-Hamadyeh covered souq. On the way to the mosque, was a short street of carpenters. Across from the mosque's side door was the gold and jewelry market. Yet another narrow alley led you to al-Hareqa neighborhood, known for its fabric and clothing markets including blankets, sheets, tablecloths and towels, or to the Bzuriyyah Souq selling spices and sweets. My aunts would often send us to buy them some candies or spices, or even better, to buy ice cream from Bakdash. Once in a while, my cousin Aida and I would go play in the massive courtyard of the Umayyad Mosque, until the guards chased us away.

My siblings and I spent a good part of our childhood and teen years at Beit Jido. With my parents constantly moving, especially during my early years, and all the tears and sorrow related to the Nakba, Damascus was my happy refuge. It provided me with stability, love, fun and even luxury. I knew that Beit Jido would always be there, at the same place, at the end of Zqaq al-Sawwaf, with the same familiar faces, noises, smells and rituals. My extended maternal family was the village that it took to raise many children, including myself.

Three seating arrangements occupied a good part of the courtyard. The *liwan*, the partially enclosed section, was reserved for formal occasions. The other two were for the not so formal, and thus had no names. When the days were especially hot, my aunts, along with their guests, would spend their afternoons at the *muraba'a juwanni,* a women's guest room adjacent to the liwan.

**Anan in the courtyard at Beit Jido, while it was
being renovated in 1999.**

Sometimes, when my aunts were having their afternoon naps, my cousin Aida and I would lie on the liwan's cool marble floor and stare at the high ceiling, captivated by its intricate geometric designs and colorful calligraphy.

"How could they reach so high and paint the ceiling?" Aida once asked.

I was wondering about that myself. But being a year older, I pretended I knew, just like my cousin Nabila.

"They must've climbed on very, very tall ladders," I said.

"Can you read what's written up there?" Aida asked, pointing to the ceiling calligraphy.

"Of course I can. See that one in the left corner? It reads, 'In the name of God the merciful.' And the one to the right reads, 'None victorious but God.' You see that writing on the opposite wall, right by the tree and the rabbit? It's a love poem, 'In the cold, she became my warmth / In the dark, she became my light.'"

As a child, I was also fascinated by the mirror on the liwan's back wall. It reached halfway to the ceiling and had a wide wooden frame, inlaid with mother of pearl. But I didn't like all the large pots of the evergreen cast-iron plant placed in the middle of the liwan. They covered the colorful marble floor and had only large green leaves, and no flowers. Every Monday evening, Fawziyeh, the housekeeper at my grandfather's house, would wash these plants, and on Tuesday mornings we, the kids, had to shine all the leaves one-by-one. Aunt Suad would inspect our jobs and often had us redo some. I asked Aunt Nahida, who loved to plant flowers, to put some in the liwan so we didn't have to shine so many leaves.

"Flowers need sun. They won't survive in the liwan."

Two large guest rooms, the muraba'a barrani and muraba'a juwanni, were located on both sides of the liwan. The muraba'a barrani, which was designated for male guests, had two entrances: one from the liwan and the other from the L-shaped *dahleeze,* or corridor, connecting the outside door to the courtyard. Guests could come and go without ever entering the courtyard. Unlike the muraba'a juwanni, which was always filled with female guests, the muraba'a barrani was hardly used, except once in a great while by my Uncle Rashad.

Carved wooden paneling in the lower qa'ah, or hall, at my grandfather's house in Damascus.

"Go open the door, these must be my guests. Be sure they enter the room from the dahleeze," my uncle would instruct.

"I know Khalo. Wallah, I know."

Although my aunts had many visitors who came for the day, the night or the week, they did not like unrelated men to come into the courtyard disturbing their privacy.

I loved spending the summers with my aunts at Beit Jido. They too must have liked having us, because my mother kept sending us every summer and most holidays. She said she needed a break from her kids. Other relatives, who lived in different cities, also came to spend time at Beit Jido. Those who lived in Damascus came every Friday to spend the day. Sometimes fifty of us would gather for the Friday feast. But nothing was as glamorous as Tuesday, the day my aunts held their weekly *istiqbal,* a day designated by women once a week, every other week or once a month to welcome female visitors in their homes. All were welcome. It must have been a great arrangement before the arrival of the telephone. But my aunts kept up the rituals for many years to come.

Aunt Suad was the family queen of etiquette and proper behavior. Being with her was like being at an all-girls finishing school. She was the one who taught us how to dress, how to walk, how to make conversation, how to set a table, how to welcome guests and how to be respectful of elders and kind to the young. She even tried once to teach me how to sing, but she gave up after a few attempts.

Khalto Suad had instructions for every occasion, and the day of her istiqbal was no exception. Before heading for her afternoon nap, she would tell us, "Today, I want all of you to have a long nap. I don't want to hear you talking, playing or arguing. Arwa and

Ayman, you sleep in my room. Aida, Anan and Susu, you go with Nahida. Maysa and Nabila, you go to the lower qa'ah."

"We know, Khalto," we would say in unison.

As soon as my aunts, Ayman and Susu fell asleep, we would quietly go out and gather in the qa'ah with my two cousins. Maysa, three years older than me, would sneak into the kitchen, bring back some ice and demonstrate for us how to keep our boobs firm by rubbing them with ice cubes.

"I want to try it. Maysa, please give me two cubes," I begged, fascinated.

"But you don't have any boobs. I do," Arwa said.

Lifting my dress, I would place the cubes on my flat chest, only to watch them slide down and melt. The water would run down my belly and get caught in my underpants.

"Look Maysa, Arwa is right. I don't have any."

"Don't worry. You're only eleven, you'll have some soon."

Nabila and Maysa were the daughters of my Aunt Isa'af. Like her mother, Maysa was funny and liked to play tricks on us. Nabila, who was four years older than me, pretended to know more than all of us. She was very beautiful, always dressed up in nice clothes and acted like a grown-up. Although she bossed us around and told us what clothes to wear, we loved hanging around her. She was the one who told us the family secrets—who was getting married, who was getting a divorce, who was having a baby and, most importantly, how children are made. My mother or aunts never discussed sex with us, but thank God for older cousins. By the time we hit puberty, they made sure we knew all about it.

After her nap and Turkish coffee, Khalto Suad would start giving us another set of istiqbal instructions.

"Go wash up and put on your nice dresses. Arwa, you help Ayman get dressed. Anan you help Susu. When the guests come, I want you to keep an eye on your brother and sister. Stay close to the kitchen and do what Fawziyeh tells you."

"We will, Khalto."

"Nabila and Maysa, since you are older, you bring the lemonade and coffee. Arwa and Anan, you empty the ashtrays and fill the nut bowls."

"We will, Khalto."

"I don't want any of you in the liwan except to do your chores. You hear me?"

"Yes, Khalto."

Although Khalto Suad had her list of what we could and could not do during her istiqbal, I couldn't wait for Tuesday to come. I treasured having all these women around. They were so beautiful and elegant, all dressed up in the latest fashions, their faces made up with rouge and red lipstick, and their eyes framed with black kohl. Defying Khalto Suad's instructions to stay away, I always found a way to hang around, eager to hear the women as they shared jokes, as well as joyful and sad stories.

The istiqbal guests started to arrive in the late afternoon and were seated on cushioned, but very stiff, wooden chairs, inlaid with mother of pearl. Matching coffee tables were lined up in front of them. Each table had a bowl of mixed nuts, a few packs of different cigarette brands and an ashtray. While the women handled the cigarettes, the children, as ordered by Aunt Suad, helped serve the food and drinks, refilling the nut bowls and emptying the ashtrays.

When the istiqbal was at its peak in the early evening, the jasmine and gardenia blooms would start opening, filling the

My mother with her four sisters, in Damascus, around 1947. *From right*: **Suad, my mother Siham, Nahida, Fariza and Isa'af.**

air with delicious scents. Kids (mostly girls) would pick up the jasmine buds and string them in necklaces to wear or to give to the guests. I would pick up a gardenia flower to give to my grandfather, who came home late on Tuesdays. My jido sat with the kids in the informal section of the courtyard, playing cards until the guests left.

"Jido, can you teach me how to play?" Ayman would beg. Ayman was the only male around, other than my jido.

"Sure, I can. Come sit next to me, let me show you."

"Jido, it is my turn. You didn't play with me," Susu would complain. He would put her on his lap and play with her.

"See, you are getting very good. You all beat me."

As we grew older, we learned that Jido let us win, and we were amazed by our discovery.

The istiqbal guests stayed almost until midnight, when a male relative—a husband, a son or a brother—came to take them home. A few spent the night. When it was officially over, the liwan and the kitchen were a mess. The hoses, buckets, floor brushes and soap would come out. Kids and adults stayed very late cleaning. My sister, cousins and I would help a bit, then get distracted playing in the fountain, spraying each other with water. We felt liberated after a long evening of behaving. The scented flowers, mixed with the cool water made all the cleaning refreshing in the hot summers of Damascus.

My aunts' istiqbal was also a source of juicy gossip. It was the place where I became aware of many family secrets. One time, while refilling some of the nut bowls, I learned that my cousin Leila had left her husband.

"We heard that your daughter Leila and her kids are staying with you. I hope she's not having another fight with her husband," Aunt Suad said.

"Sure she is. This time it looks serious," Islah said in a low voice, hoping the other women wouldn't hear.

"What's the problem?" one woman asked.

"She doesn't want to live with her mother-in-law," Islah confided, sounding defensive.

"That's awful," a third woman commented. "Where's the poor widow supposed to live if she can't live with her own son?"

"Excuse me, Islah," a fourth woman said. "I don't understand this younger generation."

"But Leila told her husband when they were still engaged, that she wanted to have her own house without his mother or any other relatives, and he agreed," said Islah, standing up for her daughter.

"Don't worry. Inshallah, they will work it out, and she will go back home soon," said Aunt Suad, trying to bring the conversation she had started to an end.

"Not this time," said Islah. "She hasn't had sex with her husband for a long time. We all know when this happens it's serious."

As the conversation got more exciting, I wanted to be sure I didn't miss anything, especially the part about sex. I took my time filling the nut bowls and wiping the coffee tables, while staying as far as possible from Aunt Suad, hoping she wouldn't notice me. But of course she did. Nothing ever escaped her watchful eyes.

"What are you doing here?"

"I'm just filling the nut bowls."

"Thank you for your help. Just go and see if Fawziyeh needs anything. And don't forget to check on Ayman and Susu. Be sure they had dinner."

"Why can't you ask Arwa. She's the older sister."

Aunt Suad gave me her hard scary look and then said, "Don't come back unless I call you. You understand?"

I was a little embarrassed to get caught eavesdropping, but was glad to have news I could share with my cousins when they came on Friday. I was wondering how much cousin Nabila knew about women refusing to have sex with their husbands.

Whenever my mother or aunts asked us to leave the room, we knew they were discussing issues children were not supposed to hear, and that included a very long list: family trouble, money, illness, death, sex, and dirty jokes.

One Monday, the day before the istiqbal, there were a lot of phone calls and hushed talk between my two aunts. When I asked Aunt Nahida what was going on, she said, "Nothing that you need to worry about." At night Uncle Rashad came, and he along with Jido and my two aunts, Suad and Nahida, went into the muraba'a juwanni and closed the door.

"Go sit with Fawziyeh. I don't want to see you until I call you," said Aunt Suad. Then she turned to Fawziyeh. "You keep these kids with you. Don't let them around here."

"What's going on Fawziyeh? Why are my aunts upset?" I asked.

"They're not upset. They just have a family matter to deal with."

"Is it about Khalo Rashad? Why is he here?"

Khalo Rashad was born after two miscarriages and four girls, and was spoiled rotten. He was tall, with large green eyes, and had a light complexion and dark hair. He and my mom resembled each other, and were equally spoiled. My uncle went to college in England and came back with an engineering degree, an English wife, and his blond daughter, Ibtisam. His other two daughters, Nawal and Sawsan, were born in Damascus. Uncle Rashad was always smartly dressed, and of course, he was a big womanizer, which drove his wife Pearl crazy.

When Khalo Rashad came that day, he hardly said hello to anyone. His gloomy face, and those of my aunts and Jido, unnerved me. Arwa and I tried to sneak out of the kitchen, hoping to hear what was going on, but Fawziyeh wouldn't let us.

The following day, my married aunts, Isa'af and Fariza, came to Beit Jido in the early afternoon. They did not seem as cheerful as usual. As soon as they said their hellos and kissed each other, my Aunt Isa'af said, "Kheir inshallah, good news, I hope! Why did you ask us to come early?"

"Let's first sit down and we'll tell you all about it," said Khalto Suad.

Once they entered the muraba'a juwanni and closed the door, Arwa, Aida and I sat in the courtyard by the cracked window, wanting to know what was going on.

"I'm sorry to have you come early, but I have some bad news I need to tell you before the guests start coming," said Khalto Nahida.

"What news? No one died, I hope?" asked Khalto Isa'af.

"No, no one died. Yesterday morning, when I was at school, I got a call from Haniya Khanum. You know her, the teacher from the English school. She wanted to ask me about a new girl in her class. Her name is Lamis Jabri. When the teacher asked her who her father was, the girl said Rashad Jabri."

"She's not talking about our brother Rashad, is she?" Khalto Fariza's voice was shaking.

"Of course she is. Why else would she call me?"

Aida looked at us and started to say something. Arwa put her hand on Aida's mouth. She didn't want my aunts to notice us.

"That can't be true," Khalto Isa'af said with confidence. "Rashad has a wife and three grown daughters. He would never, ever take a second wife."

"I said the same thing to Haniya Khanum when she told me. But when she insisted, I called Rashad, and he came over last night and told us the whole story."

"What story? He and Pearl aren't divorced, are they?"

By now Khalto Isa'af started to sound irritated and angry.

"No, they're not," said Khalto Suad, who had been unusually quiet. "Yesterday, when we asked Rashad about what we heard, he told us, 'I would have never married another woman, but I had to save my political career, my business, and of course, our family reputation.'"

"What kind of nonsense is this?" Khalto Fariza was on the verge of tears.

Hearing my aunt's cracked voice worried me. I was scared something really terrible had happened. Khalto Suad continued reluctantly.

"He told us he was having an affair with this woman—I don't even want to dirty my mouth mentioning her name—and that he got her pregnant. She threatened to go public unless he married her. You know with his high position in the government, this would be a big scandal. So he married her."

"And when did that happen?" Khalto Isa'af asked.

"Almost six years ago. He already has two girls with her."

"That bastard! And that whore. Did they think they could keep this secret forever? That Rashad, he is so selfish. Just because he has money and power, he thinks he can get away with this?" Aunt Isa'af said.

"What about Pearl? Does she know? Poor woman. That is so shameful. Wallah, I won't know where to hide my face from people once the news is all out," said Khalto Fariza, who then started to cry.

"Why are you crying now?" Khalto Suad asked. "You know

Rashad and Pearl haven't been living as husband and wife for many years."

I wanted to ask Arwa if she knew what my aunt meant by not living as husband and wife, but I was worried they would notice us.

"Suad, please don't start finding excuses for him," Khalto Isa'af responded.

"I'm not making excuses. But to be fair, for the last few years he had been telling me that he wished he could get a divorce. I told him over and over, I won't allow it. No one in our family gets a divorce."

"Poor Pearl. How can she support herself if she's divorced? She has no income and can't go back to her family in London after all these years," Aunt Fariza said.

"When Rashad came here yesterday, both Suad and I told him we won't acknowledge this wife or her kids. Pearl is our sister-in-law and her three daughters are our nieces."

"He should go tell Pearl and his daughters about this secret family of his.[14] Sooner or later they'll find out," Khalto Fariza said, starting to cry again.

At that moment, the doorbell rang and Aunt Suad said, "The guests are coming. No one needs to know about this."

Khalto Suad was the oldest of her siblings, and neither children nor adults dared to challenge her authority. She got up, quickly put on her ironed dress, some black kohl and bright red lipstick, ready to greet her guests.

Arwa, Aida and I jumped out of our seats and ran into the closest room and shut the door. We watched my aunts from the window as they came out of the muraba'a juwanni with big smiles on their faces and started to welcome the guests. "*Ahlan wa sahlan, sharraftona.* you honor us with your presence. Truly, we've missed you."

All night long, food and drinks kept coming from the kitchen located at the other end of the courtyard. First came the fresh lemonade with mint leaves, then the ice cream, delivered especially for the occasion from the famous Bakdash ice-cream parlor, only to be followed by more sweets and coffee. There was also fruit, but I don't remember where that fit in the order of things. The women talked, laughed, argued, sang and played the oud until the late hours of the night. My aunts acted happy, like nothing was on their minds.

As soon as my cousins Nabila and Maysa arrived the following Friday, I rushed to tell them the new family secret before Arwa or Aida did.

"How do you know this?" asked Nabila, disappointed that I knew a family secret before she did.

"Arwa, Aida and I heard them. All my aunts were very upset, but Khalto Fariza cried really hard," I said.

"Khalto Fariza can't have children. Maybe she's afraid Amo Abdo will marry another woman like Khalo Rashad did," said Nabila.

"I'll cut off his balls if he does," said cousin Maysa. We all laughed so hard that tears were running down our faces.

"Uncle Rashad's daughters Ibtisam, Nawal and Sawsan are coming for lunch today," said Nabila. "You better not say a word about it."

"You don't think they know by now?" asked Maysa.

"I am sure they don't. Otherwise they would've told me," said Nabila.

"Nabila, can I ask you a question before they come?" I asked.

"What?"

"I heard Aunt Suad saying that Uncle Rashad and Aunt Pearl do not live like a husband and wife. What does that mean?"

"It means they don't love each other anymore," said Maysa.

"That's not quite right," said Nabila.

At that point we heard my Uncle Rashad, Pearl and their three daughters greeting my aunts. Nabila stood up, "I will tell you what it means later. Let's go welcome them." Then she looked at me and said, "You better not say a word about what you heard."

"I won't," I said. "I promise."[15]

7. HAMMAM DAY

Damascus, 1953

"You need to go to bed now. Tomorrow is *youm al-hammam,* bath day," said Aunt Suad.

"But we're on vacation, and I'm not sleepy. Why should I go to bed now?" Arwa argued.

"Because I said so, that's why. There're so many of us taking a bath tomorrow, and we need to be done by noon."

That was during our midyear school break. My mother, my three siblings and I had arrived from Amman a couple of days earlier to spend time at my grandfather's. The two oldest daughters of my Uncle Muwffaq, Turayfa and Hanan, were staying at Beit Jido, as well. My other uncles, aunts and cousins, who lived in Damascus, were expected to join us on the following day. They always came to Beit Jido on Fridays. Thursday was the official hammam day at Jido's, a major production, especially in the winter. The only exception was the *eid,* when we had our hammam on *youm al-waqfa,* the day before the holiday. That didn't make much sense, since on the first day of the eid we were allowed to run in the streets and play outside all day. We always came back dirty and ready for another bath.

Taking a bath in the summer was not as complicated, since we showered during the week. By midday the running water, stored in large metal tanks on the roof of the house, would be really warm. People had a choice: take a warm afternoon shower or dip in the cool water of the courtyard's fountain. We chose the fountain, which we had to share with cantaloupes and watermelons that had been placed there to cool. Often we would play soccer with the melons until one of my aunts came yelling.

"Stop it now or I'll pull you out of the water."

We would quit for a few minutes, then start again as soon as the adult was gone. Even for kids, the scent of jasmine and the sound of the fountain and its cool water, which came directly from al-Feegeh spring, were so soothing and refreshing. Being in that fountain in Damascus's hot summers was just heavenly.

When I was growing up, every Damascene home had at least one faucet with drinking water coming directly from al-Feegeh, a spring on the outskirts of the city, and no drinking water could ever taste better. In Damascus, no one needed to worry about being thirsty or having cool fresh spring water, including animals. Most streets had water fountains coming directly from al-Feegeh, with a designated section for work animals, mostly horses and donkeys, which are still used in the Old City because of its narrow streets that cars cannot pass through.

In the cold winters of Damascus, we couldn't dip in the court-yard's large fountain or even take a quick shower. Winter baths were like a ritual that happened only once a week, and rarely lasted less than an hour. The ritual became even more elaborate after a woman's monthly period, as well as the day before the eid.

Once I asked my mother, "Mama, why do my aunts wash my hair and body over and over, until it hurts?"

"My sister Suad did the same to me when I was a child. It's an old tradition they inherited from the days when people didn't have a chance to bathe regularly."

"But Khaltos can bathe any day they want, can't they?"

"Of course they can. But sometimes people keep doing the same thing one generation after another, even when they don't have to."

I woke up early, just as Fawziyeh was leaving the bed I was sharing with her. It was still dark. I loved sleeping with Fawziyeh. While in the summer we had many places to sleep, during the winter, the sleeping quarter was mostly limited to four adjacent rooms on the second floor, kept warm with wood-burning stoves.

"Fawziyeh, why are you up so early?"

"I have to get the hammam going. You go back to sleep and I will let you know when breakfast is ready."

I was unable to go back to sleep. I wanted to join Fawziyeh, but it was so cold and dark, and the bed felt warm and comforting. Poor woman, she had been working day and night all week. With so many guests, including relatives and friends who came daily to see my mother, there was a lot of cleaning and cooking to do. My aunts helped only in preparing the food, while my mother thought it was a time for her to take a break from raising kids, of which she did very little. On youm al-hammam, Fawziyeh had to carry wood logs from the *abo*, a dark storage room, across the large courtyard into the hammam. She would start feeding wood into the tank until the water got boiling hot, and the hammam—a large room with cold marble floors—got very warm and steamy, just like a sauna. In the winter the hammam needed at least two hours before it was ready to welcome its first guests.

"You'd better wake up and have your breakfast before your hammam," ordered Aunt Suad as she went through the different rooms waking up the kids. Unlike Aunt Nahida, Aunt Suad was bossy. Aunt Nahida would never wake us by yelling. She would sit next to us on the bed and say, "Habibti, sweetheart, it's time to wake up."

"I'm not hungry, and I want to be bathed last," I protested.

"I said get up. I am going to the hammam right now and you better be ready when I call you."

Resentful, I got up and walked downstairs to the kitchen, where my sisters and cousins were already eating. Fawziyeh had breakfast ready: fresh warm bread, cheese, labneh, olives, olive oil, zaatar and tea.

"Come on. Your aunts are waiting for you in the hammam," Fawziyeh would say as we started talking and arguing. "Tomorrow all your aunts and uncles are coming and I have a lot to do. Finish your breakfast and go to the hammam before your Aunt Suad starts yelling."

My two aunts, Suad and Nahida, the first to go into the hammam, always bathed together. They would talk, laugh, argue and rub each other's back. They would also help bathe the children. While Aida, my Aunt Nahida's daughter, was the only child living with them, often there were other family members coming from out of town to spend the weekend or a holiday. My mother always pleaded, "Please sister Suad, please sister Nahida, can you bathe my children? I need a break."

"Of course ya habibti ya Siham, you just sleep in," Aunt Suad would say. "Take your time drinking your coffee and eating your breakfast."

My mother, twenty years younger, was the only one Aunt Suad was willing to pamper. Not having her own children, she treated my mother like her only child. No wonder my mother wanted to visit her family in Damascus as often as she could.

Once done with their own bath, my aunts would ask Fawziyeh to start bringing the kids, one or two at a time, depending on how many of the family kids they planned to bathe.

"Come on, your aunts are waiting," said Fawziyeh.

"Why don't you have Arwa go first?" I argued.

"You go now. I don't have time for this."

Not wanting to upset Fawziyeh or my aunts, I ran into the hammam. My two aunts were seated on low wooden chairs around the *guron*, a large marble water basin with hot and cold faucets. The minute I opened the door, Aunt Suad started telling me, "Anan, don't let the cold air in."

"Wallah, I swear Khalto, I came in as fast as I could."

The guron was located at the far wall facing the door, and every time the door opened, the adults would start screaming, "Shut the door, shut the door. Don't let the cold air in!"

I couldn't understand how we could enter the hammam—with its door open to a small courtyard—without letting cold air in. Poor Fawziyeh, she had to hear this so many times as she kept coming in with wood to feed the fire under the water tank, or to bring one child in or lead another one out. "How am I supposed to come in without opening the door?" she would argue.

As soon as I got undressed, Aunt Nahida would point to a small wooden chair in front of her and say, "Come here." Once she had me squeezed between her fat thighs, she would start pouring warm water on my head and naked body, saying, "Bism Allah Al-Rahman al-Rahim, in the name of God the Merciful."

Like a sacred ritual, the hammam had its own sequences. First came washing of the hair with a bar of *ghar* soap,[16] which I didn't particularly like.

"Khalto, can we use shampoo? I don't like the ghar soap. It smells rotten."

"How could you say ghar soap smells rotten? It's made of olive oil and bay leaves. No shampoo in the world is as good as ghar."

Surrendering, I would just sit there accepting my fate. Once my aunt was satisfied with the amount of foam generated, she would start rubbing my head until she was sure that the soap had penetrated every millimeter of my skull and every single hair—and I happened to have very thick hair. After rinsing my hair while using a comb to be sure that no trace of soap was left, she would repeat the washing.

"Khalto, my head hurts! Wallah, my hair is so clean now. You already washed it five times. When my mama bathes me, she only does it two or three times."

"That's your mama! Let me do it just a couple more times. Don't you want to be clean? Tomorrow all your relatives are coming to see you."

"But you do this every time you bathe me."

Ignoring my plea, she would repeat the head-washing seven times, until my hair was *zakzek,* squeaky clean. By then my skull was almost raw.

Then came the sweating part. "Go sit on the chair close to the water tank. I want you to sweat really well," my aunt would say while calling on Fawziyeh to send Arwa. After torturing my sister the same way, my aunt would say,

"Arwa, you go sit where Anan is. Anan come sit here. I think you're ready now."

As I sat back on the small wooden chair, my aunt grabbed *kees al-hammam,* a black cloth bag large enough to fit her palm into, and started rubbing my body. Dead skin started falling off. The kees, made of rough cloth, never felt nice, and if I ever complained my aunt would say, "Tomorrow all your aunts, uncles and cousins will be here. Don't you want to be extra clean? Look how much dirt you're shedding."

Truth be told, after being in the bathroom for more than an hour, being scrubbed and soaked, you would hope you're shedding only dead skin.

After the kees, came washing my body with loofah and soap, repeated two or three times. Then came the finale.

"Stand up and let me rinse you really well."

Aunt would start pouring water on my hair and body from a blessed yellow brass bowl with some religious writing on it. She would repeat this seven times, while whispering some verse from the Quran.

"Khalto, why you do wash my hair and rinse my body seven times?"

"Because seven is a blessed number, that's why."

"Blessed by whom?"

"Blessed by Allah, and his prophets," said Khalto Nahida.

"Fawziyeh, come take Anan and bring Riham in."

Fawziyeh would come in, with one hand dragging another child, and the other holding a bunch of clothes, including my underclothes. Putting those on in the steamy bath was never that easy, but my aunts insisted we put on our underwear before we left the hammam.

"Be sure to wrap her head and body well. We don't want her to catch a cold," Aunt Suad would tell Fawziyeh whenever she led a child out of the hammam. She would stop only after Fawziyeh got upset. "For God's sake, leave me alone. I raised these kids. This isn't the first time I've done this."

Wrapping me with a heavy bathrobe and a wool blanket, Fawziyeh would rush me to the warm kitchen and then up the stairway to the second level where we spent the winters.

"Here, sit by the woodstove. Put these clothes on. Stay here, we don't want you to catch a cold. You don't want to become sick."

Once she was sure I was all dressed, Fawziyeh would leave the room to attend to another child. I would lie on the diwan, listening to the crackle of burning wood, and drift into delicious sleep.

8. HERE COMES THE EID

Amman, 1954

We spent most of our holidays—*Eid al-Fitr* and *Eid al-Adha*—at my jido's home in Damascus, which was a lot of fun. Once in a while, however, we would spend it in Amman. The eid in Amman was not as festive. The street carnivals did not have as many decorations or rides, and there were very few sweets or toy vendors. But, the days leading to the eid were very exciting. At least one month before the eid, all the girls in the neighborhood and school would start taking about what kinds of dresses and shoes they would be getting.

"I'm getting a bright yellow dress," said my friend Najwa.

"My mother bought me a very pretty pink-and-white striped fabric. I already took it to Um Sarkis. She helped me chose a nice design, said my friend Fadia."

Worried I was late getting my dress fabric to Um Sarkis, I ran home.

"Mama, when are you taking us shopping? All my friends have already bought their dress fabrics."

"It's still early. We have plenty of time."

"No we don't," said Arwa. "What if Um Sarkis can't finish our dresses on time?"

"Don't worry about it. We'll go shopping soon."

Then she added her noncommittal, "Inshallah," which made Arwa and me nervous.

"Last eid, Um Sarkis asked us why we're always late getting her our fabrics," I reminded Mama. "Can't we go tomorrow?"

"This week I'm very busy at the print shop. We'll go next week."

As a child, I wished Mama was more like my friends' mothers, who took more interest in their kids, cooked them nice meals and were there when they came home from school. Instead, my mother spent most days at her print shop in downtown Amman. I don't think she enjoyed motherhood or all the chores that came with having kids. But once in a while, she would have an eruption of love and give me extra money to spend, or take me to nice stores to buy whatever my little heart desired.

"This eid I'm getting red shoes," I declared.

"Your can have either white or black shoes, so you can wear them to school," said my mother. "Besides, red shoes don't go with most clothes."

"Red goes with everything," I insisted.

"No it doesn't," said Arwa, who was more into clothes and fashion than I was.

"Then I'll get a dress to match my red shoes."

To my mother, that was reverse logic, but ultimately she went along.

"This eid, I want two dresses, like Maysa and Nabila," said Arwa, referring to our Damascene cousins.

"Inshallah."

Although I knew that meant a polite no, I was still alarmed.

"If Arwa gets two dresses, I want two, too. You always buy her more."

"That's not true." Mama insisted.

"Yes you do. Last time you bought her three sweaters and got me only one. She and Ayman are your favorites."

"I have no favorites. Arwa is hard on clothes, and she is growing fast. Her clothes don't fit her anymore."

Eid shopping with my mother was really special. It always started in downtown Amman at the fabric store.

"Ahlan wa sahlan, welcome Um Arwa. We haven't seen you in a long time. We missed you. Can I get you coffee or tea? Can I get the girls some pop or juice?" said Abu al-Walid, the store owner, as he came to the door to greet us.

"Thank you Abu al-Walid, we are fine."

"But you can't come to my store and drink nothing. Bilal, go to Abu Nader and get coffee for Um Arwa and me, and juices for the girls."

"How are you Abu al-Walid? How are Um al-Walid and the kids? I hope everyone's doing well."

"They're all fine."

Once the drinks and pleasantries were out of the way, Abu al-Walid would stand between a long table separating him from his customers and the shelves spanning the length and height of the store, filled with fabrics of all colors and designs.

"I suppose you're looking for eid dresses for your girls."

"You're right. Let's see what new fabric you've got."

Abu al-Walid would start pulling fabric rolls from the shelves behind him, spreading them on the table.

"Um Arwa, these just arrived. They're the latest fashion."

"I want this one," Arwa said excitedly.

"It's too dark for kids," my mother said, then she pointed to another. "Let me look at that one."

"Mama, I want my dress to go with red shoes. You're buying me red shoes, right?" I asked.

"Inshallah. Let's pick the fabric now."

"I want two dresses," Arwa insisted. "One blue like Nabila had last eid and another one."

"Not now. I will get you another dress later."

"You won't, you're just telling me that," Arwa said in a loud voice, which might have embarrassed my mother, but she pretended not to hear. Instead she started to look at dozens of different fabrics, asking Arwa and me if we liked this one or that.

"How about Susu?" I asked, referring to my younger sister Suad, whom I loved to dress. "Aren't we getting her new clothes too?"

"Of course we are."

"Please Mama, let me pick her dress fabric?"

"I'm going to get her and Ayman already made clothes. You can come with me when I buy them."

Once done, the owner wrapped what we bought in brown paper and tied it with a thick string.

"Ma'as salameh, goodbye Um Arwa. Give my regards to Abu Arwa. Come visit us at the house, Um al-Walid misses you."

"Inshallah we will come soon. Give my best to Um al-Walid and the kids."

Happy with our new purchases, my sisters and I each left the store smiling, proudly carrying our packets. Although Arwa was upset that my mother didn't buy her two dresses, by then she had forgotten all about it.

"Now let's go to I'zaziyeh to get your shoes," said Mama.

"Mama, can we get them from Asfour's store? His shoes are more stylish," Arwa said.

"They are not as good as Clarks," my mother insisted.

"Please Mama, let's not get Clarks this time. I want red shoes," I begged.

"Okay, but let's not make a habit of it."

The last stop was at Abu Elias's store, where we bought our underwear and socks. His was the only store in Amman that had more than plain white underclothes.

In all the stores we stopped at, we received the same offerings of coffee, tea and juices, and the same pleasantries would be exchanged. My mother knew all the shopkeepers from whom we bought clothes, shoes and food. She also befriended many shop owners in the vicinity of her print shop and knew about their families. Often she would visit the butcher shop or the bakery to chat and have coffee with the owners. But she never let them, or anyone else, forget that she belonged to a different class.

Choosing the dress design was just as exciting. Um Sarkis, the Armenian seamstress, had a shop down the street from our home. She would get really busy before Muslim as well as Christian eids.[17]

"Khalto Um Sarkis, Mama wants you to finish our dresses two days before the eid. We are going to Damascus," Arwa said.

"You're not the only one I'm making eid dresses for. If you wanted to get your dresses early, you should've brought your fabric last week," said Um Sarkis in her broken Arabic.

"I am sorry. Mama was busy. She couldn't take us shopping until yesterday. Can you please have it ready on time?" begged Arwa.

"I'll try my best. Did you pick the design?"

"Not yet."

"You better do that now."

Along with other neighborhood girls, Arwa and I would sit at

Um Sarkis's shop looking at a half-dozen European fashion maga-zines. My favorite was the *Burda*. While leafing through the catalogue, I asked Arwa to help me pick a dress

"Khalto Um Sarkis, does this design look good?" I asked.

"Anan, this one looks even better," Arwa advised, pretending to know more about fashion.

"With your fabric, this would look better," Um Sarkis said, pointing to another picture. "It's more appropriate for your age."

"But I don't want my dress to look like anyone else's. Last year you did the same design for me and Makboleh," I said.

"It's not my fault if you both picked the same design. This year no one else picked this dress. But you should go show it to your mother. Be sure to bring the magazine back quickly."

Arwa and I ran home to show our mother what we had picked, then ran back to Um Sarkis's store.

"Mama said these are fine."

"That design needs five buttons this size," Um Sarkis said, pointing to the one I chose, while handing me a small white but-ton. "Take this piece of fabric with you to help you select the right buttons, and get one or two extra. And you better get them soon if you want your dress to be ready."

Um Sarkis was short, stocky and bossy. In the morning, she looked nice with her fashionable clothes, makeup and stylish hair. But by the end of the day, with her makeup gone, her clothes wrinkled and her hair all messed up, she became even bossier. Most of us girls were afraid of her. If we ever complained about anything, she would say, "You don't like it, you can take your fabric and go to Um Hanna," referring to the other seamstress in the neighborhood. Um Hanna, an Assyrian who spoke broken Arabic like Um Sarkis, was not as bossy or pricey, but we all favored Um Sarkis because she was more stylish and had many more fashion magazines.

The few days before the eid, Um Sarkis would stay in her shop until the late hours of the night, trying to get everyone's dress finished on time. Sometimes she would ask mothers or older girls to do the final touches to their own, or their daughters', dresses. She would go around checking their work, giving them instructions. "Be careful with the hem...Not so big of a stitch... If you had brought your fabric earlier, then your dress would have been ready." Sometimes, the dresses were not ready until the morning of the eid.

In spite of her complaints, Um Sarkis did get our dresses done two days before the eid. She had them neatly folded and wrapped in heavy white paper, ready to be picked up on our way to Damascus at eight o'clock in the morning.

Arwa, Susu and I sat in backseat of my father's small car. Eager to see our new dresses, we would quietly try to open the packets, but my mother could hear the paper crackling.

"Leave the dresses alone. I don't want them to get dirty or wrinkled."

"But I want to see what my dress looks like," said Arwa.

"You had two fittings, so you know how it looks."

"Anan, did you see Nadia's and Hana's dresses? They're not pretty at all," said Arwa.

"You should see Leila's dress. It's very beautiful." I said.

"I saw it. It's not as nice as mine. I can't wait to see Nabila and Maysa's dresses. They always have the best."

As soon as we arrived at Beit Jido and said our hellos, we ran to the lower qa'ah to try on our dresses.

"Aida, where is your eid dress? Can I see it?"

The three of us, ages nine, ten and eleven, got our new clothes and shoes on, and went to show my parents and aunts our new outfits. I think I had the nicest dress. It was white, with red poppy and yellow daffodil flowers. It had matching red trim and buttons.

"You three look so gorgeous, and your dresses are so beautiful," said Aunt Nahida.

"Which one do you like the best?" asked Arwa.

"They're all very nice."

"I like mine the best," said Aida.

"How about my red shoes, aren't they pretty?"

"They're very pretty," said Aunt Nahida

"You go now and take them off before they get dirty. Don't leave them on the diwan. Hang them neatly in the closet," said Khalto Suad.

The excitement of the days leading up to eids was not limited to Muslim holidays but also included Christian ones. With all the holidays, Um Sarkis would be crazy busy sewing dresses, while the neighborhood's women would be busy going from home to home helping each other making eid cookies. Their daughters would also help, the younger ones kneading small balls of dough to keep it warm and moist, and the older ones decorating the cookies with special tiny tongs. Sitting at a large table or on a carpet around a woodstove, the women would drink coffee, chat, tell jokes and laugh, while making dozens and dozens of eid cookies. Women, regardless of religious affiliation, helped each other with their eid cookies. This happened on Muslim and Christian holidays.

Once the cookies were all done and placed neatly on large round baking trays, a mother would tell her son or daughter, "Take the cookie tray to the baker and tell him to be careful. Last time he overbaked them." Or "Last time they were not baked enough." The poor baker, he never got it quite right, but every household needed the baker. No one had an oven at home. While we, the kids, were waiting for our cookies to get baked, we would start playing, often forgetting why we were there, until the baker would send one of his helpers yelling our family names to come and take our baked cookies. In Amman, all the people made the same kind of cookies: one stuffed with dates, the other stuffed with walnuts. In Damascus, my aunts never made cookies. They ordered them from the Ghrawi sweet shop, which had a dozen different kinds to choose from.

In Damascus, we spent the eid socializing with my mother's relatives, and there were a lot of them, but I didn't know many of my jido's neighbors, except for a couple of women who used to visit my aunts. In Amman, I knew all the families on Mango Street, named after the rich Mango family who owned three large villas. But not all the families were rich. Some were like us, others were poor. We also had many different neighbors: Muslim, Christian, Chechen, Circassian, Armenian, Jordanian, Palestinian, and Syrian. But we all went to the same schools, played together, and visited each other on all the holidays. Although I spent most of the Muslim eids in Damascus, with so many different people living in our Amman neighborhood, there were always families celebrating some eid or another.

9. EID CELEBRATION

Damascus, 1954

I laid out my brand-new clothes on the diwan in the order I was going to put them on: panties, undershirt, dress, socks and shoes. This year I got a white dress with red and yellow flowers to go with my shoes. Like most eids, we were at Beit Jido.

With my clothes spread out, ready to be worn, and my new pajamas on, I went to bed. Although very tired, I kept thinking about what tomorrow might bring.

"Arwa, are you awake? Do you know how much money we'll get tomorrow?"

"A lot. We always get a lot."

"I'm so excited I can't sleep," I said.

"I can't either," said my sister.

I woke up to much commotion in the courtyard. I looked down from my bedroom window. It was still dark, but I could see my grandfather, mother and two aunts. They were all dressed up. Fawziyeh was bringing them Turkish coffee. I could smell it from my bedroom on the second floor.

"Arwa, wake up. It's the Eid!" I said.

"Leave me alone. I want to sleep."

"Look, Khalo Rashad is here with his driver, Muhyee al Deen."

I sat on the windowsill watching. Once done with their coffee, Jido said, "*Ya Allah ya kareem*, let's go. Your sisters and brothers are meeting us at the cemetery. We shouldn't be late."

Muhyee al Deen carried the white scented lilies and the *ace*, green branches, delivered the day before, and off they went to visit their dead ones. I asked my mom if I could go with them.

"No you can't. Cemeteries aren't for kids," she said.

"But I've never been to one."

"I hope you'll never have to."

I was glad Mama said no, as it was too early and I wanted to go back to sleep.

While dreaming about the carnival and all the rides in Souq al-Hamadyeh, the doorbell rang. I could hear Fawziyeh running with her *uba'ab*, wooden slippers—*click-click-click*—as she walked across the courtyard. I jumped out of bed. I wanted to be awake and dressed by the time they came back from the cemetery. I looked down from the window and saw Guzlan and Fatima, the house-keepers of my two married aunts. They always came early to help Fawziyeh get the eid feast ready. They also had to prepare breakfast to feed all those who went to the cemetery.

I was awoken by my mother saying, "*Kul sana wa inti salmeh*, Happy Eid. It's time to get up. Go brush your teeth and come join us for breakfast."

"Who's here?" I asked.

"All your aunts."

"What about Jido and my uncles?"

"They went to the Umayyad Mosque. They'll be here soon."

"Can I put on my eid clothes first? I want to be dressed before they come."

"You have time. Come have your breakfast first. Then you can wash up and get dressed."

My mother took us to Damascus for most holidays. She loved being there in her childhood home, visiting her relatives and friends, going shopping, and most importantly handing her four kids over to Fawziyeh and her sisters, who didn't seem to mind. I also liked it when we spent the eid at my jido's. I have lots of relatives on my mother's side, and they all— especially the men—gave me new money.

"How come Jido and my uncles give us more money than my aunts?" I asked my mother.

"Because they have more."

"How come?"

"Because they work."

"You and Khalto Nahida work. Do you have lots of money?"

"Not as much. Men always make more."

We were all dressed up before my grandfather and uncles came from their eid prayers. As soon as they entered the courtyard, all the kids rushed to them, wishing them a happy holiday. *"Kul sana wa inta salem*, Jido. *Kul sana wa inta salem*, Khalo." We lined up to greet Jido by kissing his hand. He patted us on the head, gave us a kiss on the cheek, and then came the new money. Our uncles were next. They also gave new money, but we didn't have to kiss their hands.

Dressed with our new clothes and with pockets filled with cash, we were ready to hit the streets looking for adventure and fun.

"Nabila, keep an eye on them. Don't let them eat too much, and be sure to be back by lunch," yelled Khalto Suad. "Arwa, keep an eye on your brother and don't let go of his hand."

Nabila was about thirteen years old, and she liked being in charge of her younger sister and her four cousins, ranging from five to twelve years old.

We ran through the narrow streets of the Old City leading to Souq al-Hamadyeh. Overnight, the *souq* had been transformed into a huge festive fair. Vendors were yelling, trying to draw customers: *"Nabet ya fool,* boiled beans, best sweets in town, fresh nuts,*"* and "Look at this car, it moves forward and backward." Their voices were mixed with hundreds of kids pleading, "Please Baba, please Mama, can you buy me this doll?" and "Please Amo, can I try this bike?" But the most exciting was the carnival area with its colorful rides. Kids lined up showing off their new clothes, arguing and bragging about how much money they got, while waiting for their turn.

After eating boiled large beans with lots of cumin, roasted nuts and cotton candy, and after standing in line for a long time, we gave up on getting on any rides and headed to Bakdash, my favorite ice-cream parlor. The place had so many rooms and it was always cool, even in the middle of a hot summer day. Aunt Nahida often brought us here. Sometimes I would place my palms and even my cheeks on the white marble table to cool off, while staring at the high ceilings, hoping to spot some birds flying. "Habibti, sit up. Don't put your face on the table, it's not that clean," Aunt Nahida would say.

"I'm waiting for the birds to fly. Khalto, how come the ceiling is so high?"

"Because this is a very old place."

"As old as Beit Jido?"

"No, not that old. Beit Abi was built in 1737, and Bakdash was built in 1855."

"How old is that?"

"Let me think. This is 1954, my baba's house is two hundred seventeen years old, and Bakdash is ninety-nine years old," said Aunt Nahida.

Nabila, holding the hands of the youngest two cousins, along with the rest of us, stood in a long line in front of Bakdash, hoping to get seated inside. The outside tables, set especially for the eid, were packed with children and families.

"We want to sit inside," Nabila told one of the waiters, who was carrying a huge tray with ice-cream servings.

"Inshallah. But we're very busy. All those people are waiting to be seated."

"Anan. Can you hold Ayman's hand? I'll be right back," said my super-hyper sister. Before I had a chance to protest, she was gone.

"Oh my God, it's almost two o'clock. We better go home right now," said cousin Nabila.

"But I want to have some ice cream," I protested.

"So many people are waiting."

"I haven't had the big wheel ride yet," said Aida.

"We have to go home now. We can come back after lunch."

"But we're not hungry," argued my six-year-old cousin Riham.

"Jido gave us lots of money, and if we don't get home before they start eating, he will be upset, and he might not give us any money next eid," said Nabila as she held the hand of my youngest cousin, Riham, and started walking home.

The extravagant eid feast was already spread out on the huge dining-room table. Two more tables were set in different rooms to accommodate almost sixty of us, not counting toddlers and babies. There was food enough for twice as many people, and the variety was overwhelming. I looked at the main table trying to decide what to eat: raw, fried, baked or grilled kibbeh, stuffed lamb, hasweh rice with minced meat and nuts, vegetable stews, fattoush, tabouli, baba ghannouj, hummus, and fried eggplant. It was hard to choose. But no matter what or how much anyone ate, my jido and aunts would keep the ritual of pushing more food. "Eat, eat. You haven't tried the *kibbeh nayee.*" "Try the lamb, it's fresh, it was slaughtered this morning." "You can't be that full." "This is different, it's a dessert, you must have some." "Just try the *burma.*" "Have some rice pudding." "Try this date cookie."

Afterwards, hardly able to breathe, the adults moved slowly from the table and collapsed into their naps, each knowing exactly which room to go to.

"You kids go to the qa'ah and sleep. I don't want to hear any noise until we get up," instructed Khalto Suad.

"Listen to your aunt," said my mother as she walked away, relieved to have someone else tell her kids what to do.

"We want to go back to Souq al-Hamadyeh," Arwa said.

"Didn't you have enough?" asked Khalto Suad.

"No we didn't," said Aida, and off we rushed back to the streets, leaving Ayman and Riham behind, while my aunt was still yelling, "Don't eat more sweets or ice cream. I don't want sick children around."

When we came home at the end of the day with dirty clothes and empty pockets, my grandfather started to question us: "Did you have fun?…Where did you go?…What did you do?…How much of your eid money did you spend?" and most importantly, "How much did you give to the poor?" After we gave our answers, he looked at each one of us and said, "That was very generous of you" or "May God bless you" or "You could have given a little more." Then he quoted some verse from the Quran about being kind to the poor: *Thy shall not oppress the orphan or speak down to the poor* or *Thy should share your God's blessing and grace.* My jido must have known the whole Quran by heart. He had a different verse for every occasion.

When we spent the eid in Amman, my father's relatives also gave us money, but not as much. "How come Amo Omar doesn't give us as much money as Khalo Rashad?" I once asked my father.

"Because he and my other relatives don't have much. They lost everything in the Nakba." Then he would remind us, "From each according to his ability, and to each according his needs."

Although I didn't quite understand what that meant, I know Baba thought that we, his children, did not need more.

Unlike Jido, my father never prayed or fasted. Neither did my mother. I don't think my father liked religion that much. But just like Jido, he did ask us how much of our eid money we gave to the poor and told us why we should. No recitation from the Quran was necessary; it was simply the right thing to do.

10. HOME REMEDIES

Damascus, summer 1956

"Come here, Sudana. Come and see what I got for you," called my grandfather as he entered the house followed by a young man carrying a large round tray on top of his head. I followed them to the dining room.

"*Shukran ya ibni,* thank you, son. Just put it here on the table." My grandfather reached into his pocket and gave the young man a few coins. I looked, and to my delight, Jido had brought me a huge tray of my favorite sweets: bite-sized thin pastries filled with pistachios called *kool wa shkoor,* which literally means "eat and thank."

"It's all yours. You don't have to share it with anyone." He looked at me for a few seconds and then added, "I want you to gain some weight this summer. You have to put on a couple of kilos before you go back to Amman. You're too skinny."

"Thank you, Jido." I bent and kissed his hand to express my gratitude.

My grandfather used to call me Sudana, a term of endearment in reference to Sudan because my olive skin was much darker than the rest of his family's. My great-grandmother was a Turkish blond, and that was my mother's family's source of beauty and pride. Even my mother, who claimed she married my father because he looked like Gandhi, would say, "My father is very beautiful; so are his seven sisters. They're all as white as milk, blond with blue eyes. Just beautiful." Unlike my mother's side of the family, I inherited my father's dark skin. Often Aunt Suad and Mama would plead with me not to play in the sun.

"Mama, where am I supposed to play? The sun is everywhere."
I didn't understand my mother. It was almost impossible to be outside and not be exposed to the sun, and playing outside was the main entertainment we kids had.

"Let her play. She's not going to be a child forever," Aunt Nahida would say. "Besides, I think dark skin suits her, especially with her bright green eyes."

When I was growing up, my Damascene relatives talked a lot about girls' and women's beauty. My older sister Arwa was very beautiful. People would say, "She looks just like Sophia Loren." My two cousins, Ibtisam—another blond with blue eyes thanks to her British mother—and Nabila, both won Syrian beauty pageants. Between beauty queens and Sophia Loren, I never felt that beautiful, at least not until I went to college.

Fawziyeh, the housekeeper at my grandfather's house, who had olive skin like mine, used to tell me, "I'm going to make you gain some weight this summer. I am going to cook all the food you like."

"I want deep-fried eggplant. It's my favorite," I said.

Every day, while Fawziyeh prepared lunch, I'd stand with her in the kitchen waiting for the deep-fried eggplant. I'd stuff it in a piece of fresh pita, add lots of salt and eat it while it was still very hot.

"Thank you Fawziyeh. This is the best sandwich I've ever had."

"You're going to spoil her lunch," my mother or aunt would yell from the courtyard.

"Leave the girl alone. For God's sake, let her eat what she likes," Fawziyeh would yell back.

"But this food is not enough for her. Look at her, she's so skinny," my mother would complain.

By the time the family sat to eat their lunch around two o'clock, I would already have eaten so much eggplant that I felt full.

"Eat, eat," my mother would beg. "You need to put on some weight."

That was almost a daily lunch ritual.

One day I overheard my mother asking her older sister Suad, "Do you think she's going to be short?"

"Siham, stop worrying. She's still young."

"She's almost twelve. Will she get any taller once she gets her period?"

"Of course she will. She'll continue to grow until she's eighteen," said Khalto Suad.

I got my period that summer. The few days before, I had terrible cramps. Everyone thought I was sick. Fawziyeh kept giving me different herbal teas, zaatar tea for a cold, mint for bad indigestion, sage for food poisoning and *maleessah,* lemon verbena, for sunstroke, but nothing seemed to work.

"Fawziyeh, Fawziyeh, I'm bleeding," I cried from the bathroom. When she saw my bloody underpants, she hugged me and said, "Mabrook, you're a woman now. How wonderful."

"What do you mean I'm a woman now? And what's so wonderful about bleeding?"

"Listen to me, now. I don't want you to tell your mom or any of your aunts about this. Not even Aunt Nahida. You hear me?"

"Why not?"

"We'll tell them later. Just not now. Not yet."

"Why not?" I asked again. Her secrecy made me anxious.

"Because I'm going to use my remedies to make you taller and whiter. Your mother and aunts don't believe in folkways, even though it works better than their doctors."

Fawziyeh had been living at my grandfather's home since I was six. She was strong and healthy, but she suffered from bad headaches. Her relatives, who lived in a small village, used to bring her leeches floating in water in a tightly closed jar. She would take them one at a time and let them latch onto her forehead to suck blood until they got fat and dropped. That was her remedy for a headache. I didn't know what to expect.

"But please, tell me first what you're going to do," I insisted.

"Stop worrying, I'll never do anything to hurt you."

"You're not going to use any leeches, are you?"

She hugged me and laughed. I, on the other hand, started to cry.

"Habibti Anan, why are you crying?"

"I don't know. I'm scared."

"There's nothing to be scared of. Come with me."

Fawziyeh put her hand around my shoulder and gently walked me down the steep stairway, across the courtyard and into the kitchen. It was early afternoon. My mother and aunts were having their nap. The sun was hot and the kitchen was stifling. She placed a low chair in the corner. "You sit here and wait," she said as she left the kitchen. Soon she came back with a heavy blanket and wrapped it around my tummy.

"It's too hot. I don't want a blanket."

"Yes you do. You shouldn't get cold when you're having your period."

I wasn't sure how you could get cold in ninety-degree temperatures, but I knew better than to argue.

Fawziyeh took a jar from the kitchen pantry, filled the kettle with water and started heating it. A few minutes later, she grabbed a bowl, put in some of the jar's content, poured in the warm water and stirred. I watched, wondering what she was going to do next.

"Here, drink this."

"What is it?"

"It's nothing. Just warm water with starch. It's going to make your skin white."

I felt nauseated at the first sip.

"Fawziyeh, this tastes terrible. I'm not going to drink it."

"It's not going to kill you. Just close your eyes and drink it fast."

I loved Fawziyeh and always did what she asked me to do. After drinking the chalky stuff, she held me from the shoulders and said, "I want you to sit up straight…yes like that…now lean your back against the wall…that's good…wrap your stomach with the blanket even tighter…now, I want you to sit still for a few minutes…I don't want you to throw up."

I sat there, nauseated and sweating, for almost half an hour.

"Please, Fawziyeh, let me lie down in my bed. I feel sick, I'm so hot."

"Stay still for just a few more minutes."

Once sure I wasn't going to vomit, she took the blanket off me and said, "Come with me."

"Where now?"

Fawziyeh held my hand and walked me to the small open space behind the kitchen. She grabbed a tall ladder and leaned it against the wall.

"I'm going to lift you up. You grab the ladder really hard and swing."

"I can't do that. My tummy hurts. I'm about to vomit."

"Of course you can. Just a few more minutes. It'll make you taller."

"Can't I do it later?"

"No. You must do it as soon as you get your first period. If you wait, it won't work."

Fawziyeh lifted me up. I stretched my arms, grabbed the ladder and started to swing.

"Please let me down. My arms hurt."

"Just a couple more swings. Later, you'll be happy and thank me."

For a whole week, Fawziyeh would wait for my mother and aunts to take their afternoon nap, then have me drink the starch and swing. By the time the week was over, I felt sicker than a dog and my arms were so sore I could hardly move. While I hated her for making me suffer for a whole week, I was grateful that her remedy for a woman's period didn't include leeches or any other strange creatures.

On the seventh day, when everyone went for the afternoon siesta, Fawziyeh got the bathroom wood-burning water tank going. She took me in and washed my hair seven times. She scrubbed my body seven times. When I was clean enough, she started pouring warm water on my head from the blessed yellow brass bowl while reciting verses from the Quran, and had me repeat them after her.

"Fawziyeh, you can't read or write and never went to school. How can you recite the Quran by heart?"

"In the village where I grew up, girls didn't go to school. My father taught me different verses."

"You still remember?"

"Of course I do. I recite some before I sleep, and when I pray."

"And you're reciting some now, as you give me a bath," I said as I hugged her. "I love you Fawziyeh, even though you made me suffer."

When the one-hour cleansing ritual was over, she wrapped me with a thick towel and took me to bed.

"Now you're so clean and warm, you're going to have a really nice nap."

"No more starch or swinging."

"No more. Go to sleep."

She gave me a big hug and walked out softly, closing the door behind her.

For the rest of the summer, I looked in the mirror every morning and stood next to Fawziyeh to see if I had gotten any whiter or taller, but nothing had changed.

"Look, Fawziyeh. You made me suffer for nothing."

"Be patient, my dear. By next summer you're going to be the whitest and tallest among all your cousins. They're going to be so jealous. You'll be happy we did that."

When the next summer arrived, I was a little taller and a shade lighter. But we were always lighter in the beginning of summer. As I entered my grandfather's house, Fawziyeh hugged me tightly, then stepped back so she could examine me carefully. I could see disappointment in her face.

"I'm sorry Fawziyeh, it didn't work," I said as I gave her another hug.

"Give it time. It'll work. I know it will," she said, and we both laughed.

To Fawziyeh's disappointment, I never got taller than five feet, three inches, and I am the shortest among my siblings and most cousins. That, along with my dark skin, gave me a good reason to continue to tease her. She, on the other hand, kept insisting that if it wasn't for her starch drink and the swinging, I would have been even shorter and darker.

11. The Baghdad Pact[18]

Amman, December 1955

It was a cold December morning. I put my coat on and was ready to walk with Arwa to school, as we did most days, when my mother said, "Arwa, Anan, if there is any trouble in the school or any demonstrations, I want you to come home. No playing in the streets or visiting any of your friends."

"Are there going to be demonstrations today?" Arwa asked.

"I hope not. Go to school now and remember what I told you. I want you to come straight home. You understand?"

"What about Ayman and Suad?" Arwa asked.

"I'm keeping them home today, just in case."

Ayman was in first grade, and Suad was still in kindergarten.

That was my first year in middle school, which was only a quarter of a mile from our home. We always walked to and from school, and often played in the streets on our way home. No parent ever drove or accompanied their kids, nor was there much concern if kids took their time getting home.

When I got to the school, older kids were gathering in one corner of the schoolyard, talking about a demonstration. Arwa and I stood by our neighbor Najla, who was in the ninth grade, wanting to know what was going on. I liked Najla. She always talked to me as if I was her age and offered me chocolates and cookies when I was at her house visiting May, her younger sister.

"Najla, my mother said something about a demonstration. Is there going to be one today?" I asked.

"Yes, a big one."

"Are you going?"

"Of course I am. As soon as the students from King Hussein High School arrive, we'll join them. You should come too."[19]

"Arwa, do you want to go?" I asked.

"No. Mama said to come straight home if there's a demonstration," my sister replied.

I was surprised by her answer. Arwa was not an obedient child; she hardly listened to Mama, or to most adults.

"We won't tell her," I said.

"Mama is already mad at me because I came home late yesterday. I don't want her to get more upset."

"You should both come," Leila interrupted. Then she added, "Be sure to leave your school bag in the classroom. Just put it under your desk. Don't bring it with you."

"What if someone takes it?" I asked.

"No one will, we always do that."

"Will the teacher let us?"

"It's not up to her. We plan to leave our bags there anyway."

Sure enough, by midmorning we heard the chanting of a distant crowd. The chanting grew louder as the demonstrators approached our school. Suddenly the students from the higher grades started pounding on our classroom door urging us to join them. As if waiting for our cues, we hurriedly packed our books in our bags, shoved them under our desks and ran out, ignoring the teacher's instructions to stay put. All it took was a few minutes for the whole school to be totally empty.

I rushed along with the rest of the students. "*Fal yasqut Helf Baghdad,*" they chanted. I had a hard time understanding what exactly the slogan meant, but I was moved by the power of our collective chanting. In one of his speeches, I had heard Egyptian President Gamal Abdel Nasser denouncing the Baghdad Pact as a "colonialist conspiracy against Arabs." I didn't understand what that meant either, but I knew that the so-called Helf Baghdad was a bad thing.

I started chanting along with the crowd: "Down with Helf Baghdad! Down with colonialism!" The more I chanted, the louder and more excited I became. Without knowing when or how, I found myself sitting on the shoulders of a man leading the demonstration and heading downtown.

As we marched along, we stopped by two other schools. More students joined us. The demonstration got bigger and louder, and the crowd became more euphoric. By the time we reached downtown,[20] other demonstrations from various parts of the city merged together to form a very large one.

I forgot all about what my mother had told me that morning until I saw the Jordanian army with tanks and big guns. Some stood in a long line, faces covered with plastic masks, hands holding clubs. Others sat on horses, watching.

Facing the army, we slowed our advance, and our chanting got quieter. Using his bullhorn, a leader of the rally announced, "We are here for a peaceful demonstration. We intend no trouble. Brothers and sisters, continue your orderly march. Do not engage in any violence."

The army moved in slowly, closing in on demonstrators and, without warning, began firing. Within seconds, the orderly and peaceful demonstration became a bloody chaotic confrontation. Organizers instructed the crowd: "Get to the ground...Run to the souq...Go to the mosque..."

People were running in every direction, their screams mixing with the sound of gunshots and exploding tear gas canisters. Suddenly I could hardly breathe, as smoke and strange smells filled the air. An uncontrollable fit of sneezing and coughing took hold of me. My eyes were on fire and tears ran intensely down my face. I wasn't sure if it was from the gas or from how petrified I felt. I ran as fast as I could up the hill and climbed the two stairways that led to our home.

My mother and other women from the neighborhood were already in the street, anxiously waiting for loved ones to come home. We lived less than a mile from where the shooting took place, close enough to hear the sounds of bullets as they screeched across the sky.

My mother ran toward me and grabbed my arm really hard.

"Where have you been? You scared the hell out of me."

"Playing with the neighbor kids," I said, trying to get away from her.

"Let me look at your face. What happened? Were you crying? Why are your eyes are so red?"

"I'm fine. I just fell down."

"Where is your school bag?"

"I left it at May's. I'll go get it later."

"Didn't I tell you...?"

"Mama, I have to go to the bathroom. I'm about to pee in my pants."

I ran inside the house, went right to the bathroom and locked the door. I didn't want my mother to ask me any more questions or see how scared I was.

Arwa, who was standing in the street with my mother, followed me to the bathroom and knocked on the door. "Anan, are you alright? Were you at the demonstration?"

I didn't answer. I washed my face and waited a few minutes for Arwa to leave, then hid in the bedroom, pretending to study. I was happy to be alone, not caring about where or what my siblings were doing.

It was about seven o'clock that evening when the doorbell rang. I rushed to see who it was. My heart dropped when I saw two police officers dressed in dark blue uniforms with guns on their waists. They were big, frowning and scary looking. Short and skinny, I looked minuscule next to them.

"Is your father home?" asked the older one. His loud voice made my heart pound even harder.

"Yes," I answered in a low trembling voice.

My father was in the study sitting at his large desk surrounded by tall wooden shelves packed with books, magazines and newspapers. That was my father's sanctuary. No one was allowed to touch any of his stuff without his permission. The only exceptions were the three volumes of the *Encyclopedia of Animals*, provided we put them back where they belonged. My father spent endless hours in his study and didn't like to be disturbed unless it was absolutely necessary.

"Baba, there are people at the door who want to talk to you."

Surprised to have unannounced guests at this late hour, he turned his swivel chair around and asked, "Who are they?"

"The police," I said, my voice still shaky.

"Speak up. I can't hear you."

"The police."

"The police? Did they tell you what they want?"

"No."

"Take them to the guest room and tell them I will be with them shortly. Don't forget to have Tuffaha make them some coffee."

Baba came after fifteen minutes, dressed up in a dark suit, a white shirt and a tie. I was eager to hear what the police had to tell him but opted to disappear to my bedroom to await my fate.

"Kheir Inshallah! Did the police tell you what they want from your father or why they're here?" my mother asked me as I walked into the living room.

"No they didn't."

I hurriedly escaped into the bedroom, the one I shared with my two sisters and brother. That was not much of an escape, since our bedroom was adjacent to the living room, where my mother sat drinking her coffee and listening to the news. Arwa was sitting in her bed playing solitaire.

"You want to play cards with me?" asked Arwa.

"No, not now"

"How about Backgammon?"

"No. I don't want to play *tawleh*."

"You're such a bore."

"Leave me alone," I said, then started to cry.

"What's wrong? Why are you crying?"

"The police are here talking to Baba. I think they're after me."

"Why? What did you do? You didn't steal or do anything stupid like that, did you?"

"No. Why would I steal? I'm not a thief," I said indignantly.

"Then why would they be after *you*?"

"They're here because I was at the demonstration."

"You're a silly crybaby. Lots of people were at the demonstration. Why would they come after you?"

The police appearance at our doorstep crushed any hope I had for my day to end peacefully. I was tired. All I wanted was to go to bed, the only place I could let go of my fear and repressed tears. But mother wouldn't let any of her kids go to sleep without dinner, which wouldn't be served for another hour.

Like a sacred ritual, all of us—parents and kids—ate dinner together in the dining room at eight o'clock sharp, every single day.

You could count on my father asking each one of his four kids, "Do you want to start?…Let's hear about your day?…What did you do?…What is the most interesting thing you learned today?…Did you have any exams?…Did you finish your homework?"

My baba was once a school principal, and he often acted like one. Once the serious talk was out of the way, he would start again, "Who wants to tell us a joke? Has anyone learned a new story today?"

I was not looking forward to our dinner chat. I dreaded my father asking me how my day was. At the same time, I didn't dare tell my mother, who was already upset that I wasn't hungry. I wasn't about to get her more angry.

I curled up on my bed waiting, trying my best not to cry. I was so scared the police were there to arrest me. I kept telling myself, *I should have listened to Mama. I wish I never went to that demonstration. Inshallah, the police will just tell Baba what I did and then leave. I'm sure Baba will convince them not to take me to jail. But what's he going to do when he finds out I lied to Mama about where I was?*

Regretful and fearful, I kept telling myself I wished this and wished that, not knowing whom I feared most, the police or my father. To him, lying was the ultimate sin.

The sound of my father's footsteps entering the living room startled me. I got up and sat at the edge of my bed, waiting. Arwa put her cards down, walked toward the door and said, "Let me find out what the police want."

"Where is Anan?" I heard my father asking.

"She's in the bedroom," my mother answered.

"Anan, come here. The police want to see you."

Anxiously my mother started asking, "What's going on? Why are the police here? Why do they want to talk to her? What happened? What could she have done?"

"Calm down, let me talk to her. Anan, I said come here."

"Okay Baba, I'm coming."

I wasn't sure my legs would carry me, but somehow I managed.

The two police officers were sitting on the couch facing the room entrance, sipping their coffees. They didn't look as scary. I dragged my feet, walking behind my father. When we entered the room Baba put his hand on my shoulder, gently pushing me to walk ahead of him.

"This is Anan," he said.

The two police officers stared at me, looked at each other, and then at my father, clearly confused.

"Are you sure this is your daughter Anan?" asked the older officer.

"What do you mean am I sure? Of course I am. What do you think, I went to the neighbors and borrowed a kid?"

"Clearly there is some misunderstanding." The officer paused for a few seconds, then asked, "Could it be her older sister? Do you have an older daughter?"

"Only one year older."

"Please accept our apologies. There must be a mix-up." The officer looked at his colleague and said, "We should leave."

"No rush. Finish your coffee." My father sounded a bit more relaxed, then he turned to me and said, "You can go now."

I felt some relief, but I knew that my unhappy ordeal was not over yet. Once the officers left, I would have to face my parents.

When the police officers left our house, I was glad to see them go without me. My relief lasted only a few minutes. When my father called me to his study and asked me to close the door, I knew I was in big trouble.

"Anan, where were you today?"

"I was at the demonstration." I was not about to lie twice in one day.

"Didn't your mother tell you to come home immediately in case of any trouble?"

"Yes Baba, she did."

"Then why did you go to the demonstration?"

I thought of a good answer and said, "Because we are against Helf Baghdad."

My father remained quiet. I could see he was trying to hide a smile, but I was too scared to trust my eyes.

"We? Who are *we*? And what do you know about Helf Baghdad?" he asked.

"I'm not sure, but I know it's a bad thing."

"Well next time, don't participate in a demonstration if you don't understand what it's about."

"Yes Baba."

"You can go now."

I left my father's study and went to my bedroom as quickly as I could, just in case he changed his mind and decided to punish me. For once, I felt lucky to be short and skinny, and look younger than my already young age.

My mother walked into the room and asked, "Are you alright?"

"Yes Mama. I just want to go to sleep."

Tears started to swell in my eyes. My mother hugged me and said, "Don't be scared. Thank God this time it turned out safe. Next time you better listen to what I tell you."

"I will, Mama. Wallah, I swear I will."

"Why don't you come and sit with your brother and sisters. It is already past eight. We'll be having dinner soon."

"I'm not hungry. Please Mama, can I just go to sleep?"

"That's fine." She kissed me, said goodnight and closed the door.

Fully dressed, I lay in my bed. The shooting, the blood, the screams and the police all came to haunt me. I covered my head and cried like never before.

**Our family at home in Amman, Jordan, in 1956.
My older sister Arwa (*left*) and myself (*right*) are
beside my parents; my younger brother Ayman
and sister Suad (Susu) are in front.**

12. My Magic Box

Amman and Damascus, 1956–1957

"You should see the transistor radio my mother bought. It's so small but has as many stations as the big radio in the living room," said my cousin Aida as soon as we arrived at my jido's house in Damascus. It was the summer of 1956 and I was eleven years old.

"Where's Khalto Nahida?" I asked.

"She's in the kitchen getting lunch ready. She's making fried eggplant, your favorite."

I ran through the courtyard, eager to see my aunt. I was just as eager to see this transistor radio Aida had been talking about. She even sent me a letter in Amman describing it. The familiar scent of jasmine, mixed with the aromas of fried eggplant, fresh bread and roasted lamb filled the courtyard. All of a sudden I felt very hungry.

"Marhaba, hello, Khalto. We're here."

"Ahlan wa sahlan, welcome, I've missed you," said Khalto Nahida as she took me into her big bosom. "Where are your mother and siblings?"

"They're here, bringing all the stuff in."

"Let me wash my hands and go greet them."

My aunt had the radio on the kitchen counter. She was listening to the news. I stood there looking at it with so much amusement. As soon as my aunt left the kitchen, Aida started to play with it, changing from the news station to music.

"Oh my God, please Aida, don't change this station. I love Abdel Halim Hafeth. He's my favorite singer. Do you like him?"

The Egyptian romantic singer Hafeth was the Frank Sinatra of the Arab world, adored by millions of young people, especially girls and women.

"But I want to show you how many stations this small radio has," said Aida.

"Let me hold it. Let me try changing the stations," I said.

Before I had a chance to hold the radio, Khalto Nahida walked into the kitchen.

"Aida, how many times do I have to tell you not to touch it?"

She took the radio from her daughter, placed it back on the kitchen counter and turned it to a news station.

"Khalto, Aida has been telling me about your transistor radio. Can I see it? Please? Can I carry it?"

"No. It's not a toy. If you want, you can sit next to me and listen to it."

Khalto Nahida was a softie. All it took were two kisses and a big hug for her to give in and let me have it. The radio was light and small, no larger than a shoebox. I would hold it with both arms close to my chest and walk around the courtyard fountain listening to different stations. I wouldn't let go until my aunt finally insisted.

"Give me the radio. You've had it enough. I need to listen to the news. Be careful. Don't drop it."

When my aunt took her afternoon nap, my cousin Aida and I would sneak into her bedroom and take the radio to test if it worked in different parts of the house—and it did! Before Khalto bought her transistor radio, the whole family had to sit in one room around the large radio to listen to the news or to music. Whenever we kids made any noise, one of the adults would say, "Stop talking, we're listening to the radio," or "Go play outside. We want to hear the news." As I was not yet twelve, I wasn't that interested in the news, which was mostly about Israel, the Palestinian refugees and the new Egyptian president, Gamal Abdel Nasser.

One afternoon I sat with my Aunt Nahida while she was packing. She was leaving the next day for Ba'abdoun, a Lebanese resort that she and her friends used to go to every summer. I never liked it when she was gone, leaving us with Aunt Suad, who was strict with kids. And that summer, I really did not want to see her leave. I was afraid she would take her radio with her.

"Khalto, are you going to take the transistor with you?"

"Of course I am."

"Can you leave it here? Please? I promise I'll take care of it."

"No habibti, I want to take it with me. That is why I bought it."

When I went back to Amman, I could not stop telling my friends about my aunt's radio.

"You should see it. It's very small, you can carry it in one hand. It's called a transistor. It has many stations and it works like magic."

Nor could I stop asking my father to buy me one.

"Baba, please, can you buy me one now? You don't have to buy me anything for my birthday."

"You don't need a radio. It'll keep you from studying," he would say. "Books are better for you than a transistor."

Since my father loved books so much, he thought that we should love them, too. He spent most of his time reading in his study and would get upset if we made loud noises: "Be quiet, I'm reading," or "I'm writing."

Unlike my father, my mother liked to go out, to socialize and to travel.

"Your baba, all he does is sit and read. He doesn't want to go anywhere or visit anyone. He just consumes one book after the other. He's so boring."

I was not a particularly demanding child, but once I saw Aunt Nahida's transistor, I never stopped wanting one. It took a whole school year of begging, and even crying, before my father finally gave in. While I wanted a transistor radio so bad, Arwa, on the other hand was nagging Baba to buy her a bicycle.

"I see you've done well in all of your classes," said my father when I proudly handed him my seventh-grade end of year school report. He started reading it aloud. "Writing and Composition: 'excellent'; Reading: 'very good'; Grammar: 'good'; Math: 'very good'; History and Geography: 'very good'; Religion: 'fair.' This is a good report, Anan. I'm glad the only fair grade you got is in religion. This summer you need to work on your grammar."

"I will Baba, I will," I said.

Next, he went over Arwa's report. He read it aloud, as he'd done with mine. Then he said, "You, too, did very well. I'm so proud of you both." Finally he added, "Guess what I'm going to do this week?" His face was smiling and his voice was soft.

"What Baba, what?" Arwa and I asked.

"This afternoon, I'm going to take Arwa to buy her bicycle. And the day after I'll take you to get your transistor."

"Baba, say this again. Say *wallah.*"

I couldn't contain my happiness. But then it dawned on me that he was taking Arwa first.

"Can we all go together this afternoon?"

"Let me take Arwa today, and I'll take you tomorrow. That way we don't have to rush."

I wasn't happy he was taking Arwa first. But I was so thrilled about getting my radio, I didn't want to argue.

When Arwa came back with her bicycle, Ayman, Suad and I, along with a dozen of the neighborhood kids, met her in the street to look at what she got. Arwa was so proud of her new bike, she allowed us to look at it for a few minutes. As soon as she brought it to the house, she started to practice on our very long veranda, holding onto the rail.

"Arwa, please let me try it," I begged.

"Not now. I need to learn how to ride it."

Sure enough, Arwa kept at it, falling a few times until she was able to ride it.

"Please Arwa, can I try it now?"

Arwa ignored my plea and ran to the street with the bike, while Ayman, Suad and I ran after her. The neighborhood kids came back asking if they could try it. She said no to all of us, got on her bike and took off.

The following day my father said to me, "This afternoon is your turn, Anan. You and I will go downtown after my nap."

I was overjoyed. Not only was I going to get my radio, I was also going shopping with my father, a rare occasion in our household. Shopping was my mother's chore. That was the second day of our summer break, and as it turned out, it was the happiest day of my childhood.

My mother, who did not particularly like cooking, made a special lunch for us, to celebrate the end of the school year.

"Look what I've made, chicken with *hashwe* stuffing," she said proudly.

"Thank you, Mama. It smells really good," I said. While I loved the hashwe made of rice, minced meat and roasted nuts, the excitement of that afternoon made me lose my appetite.

After lunch, my parents went to their bedroom for their afternoon nap.

"Baba, are you going to sleep long?"

"Not really. We can't go anyplace until the stores are open. You know they all close for lunch."

"What time are we going?"

"Around five."

It was only two-thirty. I washed up, put on my newest dress and my nice sandals and sat in the living room, waiting. I tried to stay busy reading and playing cards with my sister, but I couldn't concentrate. I ran to my parents' bedroom as soon as I smelled the Turkish coffee.

"I'm ready to go, Baba."

"I see you are all dressed up. Let me drink my coffee and get dressed. Then we can go."

My father took his time getting ready. Although we were going downtown, Baba had to put on a dark suit, white shirt and a tie. He always dressed like that, even in the hot summers of Amman, or when we had guests over.

I sat next to Baba in his black Vauxhall car, and off we drove to downtown Amman. The Bishara store on Salt Street was very small but packed with stuff—radios, irons, toasters, washing machines and vacuum cleaners.

"Baba, where are the transistors? I don't see any."

"Don't worry. I know he has them. Here they are," he said, pointing.

On the shelf behind the counter, where the owner was standing, were a few transistor radios of various sizes. After exchanging a few pleasantries, my father said, "This is my daughter, Anan. I want to buy her a transistor because she did very well in school. Anan, say hello to Amo Abu Hani. Go ahead, shake his hand."

"You're a lucky girl," said Abu Hani. Then he turned to my father and said, "I have a few models, mostly American. But I have a couple of Japanese models, too. What kind of a transistor do you want?"

"Show them to Anan. Let her choose the one she likes."

The owner, whom I had never seen before but had to call Amo, started bringing out the radios one at a time. He would put two or four batteries in, depending on the radio's size, and turn it on.

"This one is American—Zenith. It's the best. Listen, it sounds really good, doesn't it?"

"Amo, can I look at that small one?" I asked.

"This one is Sony. It's Japanese. It just came out but is very good."

"Look Baba. This is beautiful! Amo Abu Hani, how much is it?"

"Don't worry about the price. Just choose the one you like. This is your gift for doing so well in school," my father said.

"Can I carry it? Can I change the station?"

"Go ahead," said Abu Hani.

After examining it and changing the dial to a few stations, I put it back on the counter. Pointing to a smaller one, "Does that one, the one with a leather jacket and a strap, sound as good as this one?" I asked.

"This one is Phillips, it's American-made, even better but more expensive."

"It doesn't matter, let her look at it," said my father.

"Baba, this is the one I want. Can I have it?

"Of course you can," he said, reaching into his back pocket for his wallet.

"Mabrook, this Phillips is the best radio I have," said Abu Hani. "Here you go, take two batteries, my gift to you."

"Thank you Amo Abu Hani," I said, eager to leave.

"Baba, Amo Abu Hani said that every radio we looked at was 'the best.' Is the one I got the best?"

"He's a businessman, he wants to sell. The one you picked is very good and very beautiful," said my father.

"Baba, can we hurry? I want to get home and try it. I want to show it to Mama, my sisters and brother. I also want to show it to my friends. Thank you, Baba. I love you. You are the best baba ever."

When I got home, Arwa, Suad and Ayman, gathered around me as I changed the stations, each begging to hold it.

"I will let you use my bike if you let me borrow your radio. I want to listen to "*Ma Yatluboho al-mustameo'un,*" listener's requests.[21] They always have Abdel Halim Hafeth. He's my favorite."

That night I couldn't sleep. I kept turning the radio from one station to another and going to different parts of the house to see how it sounded. I stayed up until one. By then, every single station had said goodnight to its listeners.

After getting my radio, I didn't read as much. Instead, I would stay up really late listening to my radio. My favorite station was *Huna Al-Qahera*, This Is Cairo,[22] which had lots of soap operas and love songs by my favorite singers. Sometimes I would listen to Damascus radio, which also played love songs into the late hours of the night.

During that summer, Arwa spent most days on her bike, going up and down the street, trying to learn new tricks, like jumping her bike or riding on the back wheel. Kids would watch and pester her to lend them the bike.

"You can have it for ten minutes in exchange for an ice cream or chocolate bar."

Arwa was a tough girl, and no kid in the neighborhood—boy or girl—dared to take one more minute than the allotted time, or not give her what she asked for.

One evening, I was sitting on the veranda diwan next to the jasmine tree my mother had planted when we moved into the house, enjoying its delicate scent, while listening to my radio. Arwa, who was practicing jumping her bike for a few days, was at it again.

"Look Anan. I really can fly my bike almost a full meter. Why don't you lie on the floor and I'll ride real fast and then jump over you without my bike even touching you."

"You're crazy. Why would I want to do that?"

"Don't worry, I've been practicing. I'm really good at it."

"Go jump over a piece of wood."

After she gave up on convincing, me she tried Ayman.

"How would I know you can do that?" Ayman said.

"Wallah, I won't hurt you."

"Let me see you do it first. Do it with Suad."

Luckily, Mama came out at just the right moment to the veranda where Arwa had laid Suad on the floor and was about to try her acrobatic bike trick.

"What the hell are you doing? Oh my God! Susu get up! How did I end up with such a crazy daughter?" my mother said, shaking her head while helping Suad get up off the floor.

On the other hand, I spent the days with my radio, standing outside the doorway of our home, strategically located in the middle of the block. Or, I would walk up and down the street with my radio hanging on my shoulder, turning it up loud enough for every kid in the neighborhood to hear it. I wanted the whole world to see and hear my radio. Kids would gather around, asking me to change the station and listening with amusement and fascination. I would only lower the volume when I saw my father's car approaching, or when I got a certain look from the older women, who felt they had the right to discipline every child in the neighborhood, whether they were related to them or not.

At first, my radio was no more than a toy that increased my popularity and prestige among the boys and girls in our neighborhood. We would spend hours listening to passionate Egyptian soap operas and the romantic songs of Fairouz, Shadia, Asmahan and Abdel Halim Hafeth. Although adults avoided talking about love and lust with us or around us, love songs were played at home, at the stores and in taxis. People listened to them day and night. Thanks to my radio, we were able to listen to them even when we were hanging out in the streets or in some neighbor's backyard. In no time, I became one of the most popular kids in the neighborhood.

~

A few months after I got my radio, adults started talking about war and about the Egyptian leader Gamal Abdel Nasser. I even heard my parents talking about possible war. "Nasser is going to nationalize the Suez Canal," my father said.

"He should," responded my mother. "The canal belongs to the Egyptian people, not to England or France."

"I bet you Britain and France are not going to like it. I'm afraid they will attack Egypt."

Talk of a possible war dominated most adult conversations and all the news. Suddenly we weren't kids anymore. Thanks to my transistor, like adults we started to listen to nationalist songs, to Nasser's long speeches and to the Egyptian commentator, Ahmed Said.

"I bet you Nasser could defeat England and France put together," I told my friends after we listened to one of his speeches.

"I bet you he can," said my friend Najwa.

As I grew older, my radio assumed a new function: to separate the neighborhood kids. There were "us," the good kids, or the nationalists, who loved Nasser; and "them," the bad kids, or the reactionaries, who loved King Hussein. We, the good kids, would gather on a balcony, in a room, a backyard or on a street corner to listen to my radio. From that small box we learned about Arab nationalism, African unity and the Non-Aligned Movement. From my radio, we learned about revolutionaries around the world. We learned about Uncle Mao, Patrice Lumumba, Castro and Che, and we learned about Martin Luther King and Malcolm X. Through my small radio, I felt a bond uniting me with all these people around the globe. I did not know how the bond worked, but I learned it from my radio, my magic box.

Detroit, 2010
I held my radio in my hands, tuned in to my favorite station and turned the volume up, but it didn't respond. I smiled.

"You're not taking this to the new house in Ann Arbor, are you?" said my husband Noel, as he was getting dressed to go to work.

"Of course I am. This is a precious radio with lots of memories. I can't leave it behind."

"It's nothing but a piece of junk. Just throw it out."

"One person's junk is another's treasure."

I rewrapped my small Phillips radio with my silk scarf and placed it safely in a drawer next to my bed. I often check on it, hoping it will work. I even expect to hear some of the fifties songs.

"I don't understand why you're holding on to this ugly thing while you're getting rid of more valuable stuff," said my husband.

"You should've seen it when it was new. It was just beautiful. It used to have a brown leather jacket and a long strap."

"That was a hundred years ago. Look at it, it looks like it's been to more than one battlefield."

My husband was right. We were moving from Detroit to a smaller house in Ann Arbor. My radio was really old, and it didn't work. Its leather jacket was long gone, and so was its strap. It even had duct tape over the plastic cover that held the batteries in. I did try to fix it more than once, but was told by every repair shop, "Throw it out, it is not fixable."

But I will fix it one day. I know I will.

13. *LATEEFEYEH*[23]

Amman and Damascus, 1958–1959

Three days after the school year ended, my mother called Hussein, a distant relative who owned a taxi.

"I want to send the kids to Damascus. Are you free any day next week?"

"Inshallah, I can take them on Tuesday."

I often wondered if my mother really loved us or enjoyed having kids. As far as I can recall, she shipped us, her four kids, to Damascus whenever she could. Once, I mustered up the courage to ask my father, "Baba, do you think Mama loves us?"

"How could you say that? Of course she does."

"How come she keeps saying 'I need a break from the kids,' and keeps sending us to Beit Jido?"

"It's hard for any mother to take care of four kids and work at the same time. I thought you loved going to Damascus."

"I do. It's fun. I have lots of cousins to play with."

My brother Ayman was nine at the time, and I was thirteen. Unlike us girls, he wasn't that thrilled about spending his summer in Damascus.

"Mama, this summer I don't want to go to Beit Jido," Ayman said.

"Why habibi? You always have a good time when you go there."

"No I don't. There's no one to play with."

"What do you mean there is no one to play with? You have your three sisters and all your cousins."

"They're all girls."

"What difference does it make? They all love you and like to play with you."

"No they don't. Please Mama, can I stay?" Ayman begged.

Although my mother vehemently denied it, she couldn't say no to Ayman, her only son.

"*Pasha habibi,* [24] of course you can. But you can't stay home or play in the streets all day long. Some days you'll have to come with me to the print shop.[25] At least half days."

"Can I stay, too?" Susu asked.

"No habibti, you go with your sisters. Anan will take care of you."

Mama was right. I did take care of Susu. But when it came to poor Ayman, I just didn't want to do anything with him. Once in a while my mother would ask me to help him with his schoolwork or make him a sandwich. I would protest, "Why should I? Just because he's a boy?"

"No, not because he's a boy. Because he's your younger brother. You help Susu all the time, don't you?"

So, for the first time, my two sisters and I went to Damascus to spend the summer without my brother. After we had been there about a month or so, Khalto Isa'af came to Beit Jido very early. My two aunts, Suad and Nahida, were still in their nightgowns and drinking coffee in the courtyard. The smell of jasmine and coffee, mixed with cardamom, filled the cool fresh morning air.

Khalto Isa'af lived in the modern upscale Salhiyyeh neighborhood, more than an hour's walk from my grandfather's house. She cared a lot about her figure and often took a morning walk all the way to visit her sisters. Like her daughter Maysa, she had a great sense of humor and enjoyed playing tricks on people.

My aunts got up and hugged their sister. They kissed on both cheeks twice, saying, "Ahlan wa sahlan. Ahlan wa sahlan. Wallah we missed you!"

As soon as they settled down, Aunt Suad said, "What brings you here this early? Did you walk?"

"No. I took a taxi. I've been up for hours listening to the news about Iraq."

"Kheir inshallah. What news?"

"Didn't you hear what happened? There's been a military coup. King Faisal and his uncle Abdel el-Ilah have been killed."

"You're kidding, aren't you?"

"No, wallah it's true."

"Go tell Fawziyeh to make us fresh coffee," Khalto Suad told me as the three sisters hurried into the muraba'a juwanni, the large living room adjacent to the courtyard, where the big radio was. I ran to the kitchen and ran back, wanting to know what was happening. My aunts sat listening to the news for the rest of the day. I would listen for a while, then go read or talk to my sisters or Aida, only to soon come back, eager to listen to more news.

Khalo Rashad came over that evening to tell Aunt Suad that he wanted to have his Hizb al-Shaab [26] meeting next Monday. My uncle was the head of the Syrian People's Party and had meetings at Beit Jido on the first Monday of the month.

"This is your home as much as it is mine. But didn't you have your meeting last week?"

"We did, but we need to have an emergency meeting to address the situation in Iraq. This is definitely the doing of Nasser and the communists. The Jordanian government declared a state of emergency and is arresting lots of people."

"The military coup is in Iraq. Why would they arrest people in Jordan?" asked Khalto Suad.

"Just precautionary measures. After all, King Faisal is the first cousin of King Hussein. Only a few months ago, the two countries established the Arab Federation of Iraq and Jordan. King Hussein has every right to be concerned."

When I heard Khalo denounce Nasser, I sat there listening quietly, hoping no one would notice my presence or ask me to leave. I was not yet fourteen, but I had already developed an interest in politics, and I loved the Egyptian leader, Gamal Abdel Nasser.

"We should call Siham to check on her," Khalto Suad told her brother.

"I've already tried. The phones between Jordan and Syria have been disconnected."

I ran to the qa'ah to tell Arwa and Susu what I'd heard; then the three of us ran back to my aunts and uncle. "Are my parents going be all right? I want to go home. I want to be with them," Arwa said.

"You don't need to go home or be concerned. Your family is going to be just fine," said Khalto Suad.

Susu, who was only seven, sensed our anxiety and started to cry.

"I want to go home, I want to go to my mama and baba."

I hugged her and said, "Don't worry habibti, we'll go home soon. Right Kahlo?"

"Inshallah," he said, with a sarcastic half-smile.

"Khalo, why did you say inshallah? You don't think my parents will be okay?" I asked.

"Of course they will. You don't have to worry. Just enjoy your summer vacation. Then he looked at Khalto Suad and said, "Ibtisam is going to Beirut for a couple of days to visit her friend. She can take the girls and drop them at Amti Um Mumdooh's. Let them enjoy the beach." Then he looked at Arwa and said, half-kidding, "Be sure your sister Anan doesn't sit in the sun. She doesn't need to be any darker."

"Khalo, how am I going to be at the beach and not get any darker? It's not my fault I'm not as blond as your daughter Ibtisam," I said teasing.

"We better ask Amti Um Mumdooh and her daughter Fardous if they can have so many kids at the same time," Khalto Suad said.

"What do they care? They have a big house and a couple of servants," Khalo Rashad responded.

I turned to Aunt Nahida and said, "Khalto, can we go?"

"Of course you can."

"Can you buy me a new bathing suit? The one I have is old."

"I'll get you a new one before you go."

"How about me?" Susu said. "I need a new one, too."

"Mama, can I go with them?" Aida asked.

"If you want to."

"Can I get a new bathing suit, too?"

"I'll take the four of you and get you what you need."

Arwa, who had been unusually quiet, told my aunts, "I don't want to go with them."

"Why?" asked Khalto Suad. "You'll have a good time at the beach with your sisters and Aida."

"I want to go stay with Khalto Isa'af. I want to spend time with Maysa and Nabila," she said, referring to my aunt's daughters. Arwa, who was only a couple months short of her fifteenth birthday, had blossomed early and looked much older than I did. She preferred to spend her time with our older cousins. Also, unlike Susu and I, Arwa did not get along with Aida.

"As you like," Khalto Suad said.

"But I want to go shopping with them. I need clothes and shoes."

"Tomorrow, inshallah, I'll take the four of you."

Khalto Nahida loved kids. She was always ready to take us places and buy us whatever we asked for, ignoring her older sister's advice: "You spoil these kids. It's not good for them."

~

On Monday, the day my uncle was supposed to have his People's Party meeting, Khalto Suad gathered cousin Aida, my two sisters and me to give us her instructions.

"This afternoon, my brother Rashad is having his meeting. I want you to eat your lunch early and have your nap in the upper qa'ah. Anan, you keep an eye on your sister Susu. Arwa and Aida, I don't want to hear you fighting or arguing, and I don't want any of you to come down until the meeting is over. You understand?"

"But didn't he have his meeting last week?" Arwa asked.

"He is having another one today."

"What if we need to go to the bathroom?" asked Aida.

"You come down quietly and go to the bathroom by the kitchen. But don't let Khalo Rashad see you."

"And what if he does? I live here. I can't just disappear." Aida did not like Uncle Rashad that much. He often complained about her, telling my aunts, "That girl is too spoiled. You let her have whatever she wants, and come and go as she pleases."

"If you want your uncle not to complain about you, then you do what I tell you," said Khalto Suad.

"He will complain about me no matter what. He doesn't like me because I'm adopted. I am not a real Jabri." Aida was almost crying.

"You are our daughter and I don't want to hear you say this ever again. And you need to have some respect. After all, he is your uncle."

"Aida, why do you say you're not a real Jabri? Of course you are. You are my favorite cousin," I said, giving her a hug.

When we stayed at Beit Jido, we saw Khalo Rashad every Friday and once a month on Mondays. On Fridays he came with his British wife, Pearl, and their three daughters, Ibtisam, Nawal and Sawsan. All my jido's other children and their families also came for the Friday feast. Uncle Rashad came again by himself on the first Monday of the month, along with his driver Muhyee al Deen, to hold his political meetings. While we were having our naps, two or three men would come to help Muhyee al-Deen set up. They would move dozens of plant pots to the storage room, set up chairs theater style and brew large pots of sugarless Arabic coffee. Members of the People's Party would start arriving around four o'clock and stay for two or three hours, passionately discussing politics. Occasionally, Khalo Rashad would give a short speech.

Once party members started to arrive, the courtyard was off-limits to all women and children. After their naps, my grandfather would go back to work, and my two aunts would retreat to the muraba'a juwanni. We, the children, had to find a way not to be seen or heard. But because all the windows of the house looked out onto the courtyard, we could watch and hear what was going on from the second floor.

On the Monday after the Iraqi coup, more people came to the meeting than usual. Muhyee al-Deen kept adding chairs and making more coffee. The courtyard was packed with men sitting and standing. Later that day, Khalo Rashad was telling Jido that at least one hundred fifty men came to the meeting. "*Allah yehmeek ya ibni*, may God protect you my son," said Jido.

During the meeting, I sat on the windowsill of the upper qa'ah, listening. My khalo gave a short speech.

"The situation is rather grave. This is Nasser and the communists' doing. Our allies are with us, and King Hussein already asked for their support. Great Britain and the US are watching the situation closely. They are not going to sit idle while the influence of the communists and Nasser spread. The Jordanian government is arresting communists, socialists, Arab nationalists, Baathists and their sympathizers. Although we value democracy, this is an emergency, and the Jordanian government must take all necessary measures."

I was getting very upset listening to my uncle. Not only did I love Nasser, and had recently sent him a letter, but I also knew that my father was one of those socialist sympathizers my uncle was talking badly about. Once the meeting was over, and my uncle and all his people were gone, I asked Aunt Nahida if my baba was going to be safe.

"Don't worry, he is going to be safe. Your baba has a high post in the government and everyone respects him. You know that, don't you?"

"I do," I said, although I wasn't totally convinced.

"Khalto, why was Khalo Rashad speaking badly about Nasser?"

"Because he doesn't like him or agree with his politics."

"Why not? Everyone likes Nasser."

"No, not everyone. Definitely not your uncle," said my aunt.

"I adore Nasser. I already sent him a letter telling him how much I admire and love him. Do you think he'll get it?"

"He might. But you better not let your uncle know about it."

I will never forget the day I got a letter from Egypt with a signed picture of Nasser. I rushed to my aunts, yelling:

"Khalto Suad, Khalto Nahida! Look what I got—it's from Nasser! It says *Dear Anan* and it has his signature! He read my letter and signed the photo. Look!"

Khalto Suad reached out her hand to me and demanded, "Let me see it."

I handed her my new valuable possession, feeling very proud.

"How did you get this?" she asked, after looking at it closely and turning it back and forth.

"I wrote Nasser a letter and he wrote back."

"Well, you better not let your Uncle Rashad see it."

"Why not?"

"Because I said so."

No wonder Aida doesn't like Uncle Rashad. She probably knows him better than I do, I thought to myself while telling my aunt, "Okay, Khalto. I will keep it in my bedroom."

Toward the end of August, my aunts told us that the borders between Jordan and Syria were still closed, and the phones were still disconnected.

"Your mother sent a message to enroll you in schools here. No one knows when the borders will reopen," said Khalto Suad.

"How could she send a message if the phones and the borders are closed?" Arwa asked, not quite believing her.

"She called my aunt, Um Mumdooh, who called us this morning."

"I don't want to go to school here. I miss my mama and baba and I miss Ayman. I want to go home," Susu said, then she started to cry.

"Come here habibti. Don't cry. You'll be going to school with me. Don't you like that?" Khalto Nahida said.

Susu walked to my aunt and sat in her lap. "Khalto, will you be my teacher?"

"No, I won't. But you'll have many nice teachers. They're all my friends."

"But I miss Mama and Baba."

"I miss them, too. Inshallah you don't have to stay the whole school year. As soon as the borders open, you can go back to Amman. But for now you have to be in school."

"But what if I don't want to go to school here?" Arwa asked.

"You know how strict your parents are when it comes to your education," said Khalto Suad with a firm voice, clearly wanting to end the discussion. At that time Arwa was going into ninth grade, Susu into second, and I into eighth.

The fear of never seeing my parents again, a sensation I felt when I was left at my jido's in 1948, came back with a vengeance to haunt me.

"But what if the borders never open? What if I never see my parents and brother again?" I said. Then I began to cry. Susu started to cry, too.

"Ya habibti ya Anan, why are you crying? Look what you did. Now Susu is crying again. You're with us and we love you. Inshallah the borders will open very soon. Come here, come sit next to me." As I did, she hugged me and whispered in my ear, "Tomorrow we can go to Souq al-Hamadyeh to buy you and your sisters new shoes and school uniforms. Then we can go to Bakdash and have some ice cream."

~

A few months later, I came back from school to find some of my aunt's women friends at Jido's house. Later that evening, more women arrived. They were planning to spend the night.

"How many women do you expect to come tomorrow?" asked Rasmyieh Khanum. She was my Aunt Suad's best friend, and I had heard rumors they were lovers.

"Let me see. Hajje Zahra, my sisters Isa'af and Fariza, Muhebeh Khanum is coming and bringing her two sisters, Fatima and Um Ahmed, and Shahira and Insaf are coming too," said Khalto Suad. Shahira and Insaf lived together. I had heard that these two were lovers, as well.

"Khalto Suad, tomorrow is not your istiqbal, so why are all these women coming?" I asked.

"Tomorrow we are going to have *Lateefeyeh*. These women are going to help us."

"Khalto, what is Lateefeyeh?" Arwa asked.

"It is a religious ritual. We read a sura from the Quran and then say *ya lateef* twenty thousand times."

"Twenty thousand times? That's a lot!"

"It is. But if we have lots of people, we can do it in one day."

"And why 'ya lateef'? What does that mean?"

"We call on God the Merciful. We ask him to have mercy on people we love."

"We are doing this for your baba," said Rasmyieh Khanum.

Khalto Suad stared at Rasmyieh Khanum, as if warning her not to say more.

"Why are you doing this for Baba? What's wrong with him? Is he sick?" Arwa asked, sounding scared.

"No, he's fine," said Khalto Suad.

"Say wallah, you swear," Arwa insisted, while I sat there quietly trying to figure out what they were talking about.

"I told you he is safe. It is something we do for all the people we love. Now you go wash your hands, have a snack and do your homework. Tomorrow morning the rest of the women are coming. After breakfast we will start the Lateefeyeh. I want you and Anan to do this with us."

"How about me, can I do it too?" Susu asked.

"No, you're too young. You and Aida will go to school together."

"How about us? We have school tomorrow. Besides, I don't know what you're doing," I said.

"Your Aunt Nahida got you and Arwa permission from your teachers to skip one day. We need your help. Remember to wash before praying. You must be clean to do this."

"I don't know how," I said.

"I don't either," Arwa said.

"*Ya eib alshoom alaykum*, shame on you. Your parents should have taught you. I have to talk to your mother when I see her. *Wadu* washing ritual is simple. Fawziyeh will teach you. Also, be sure to wear your pants. I don't want you wearing short dresses. You need to dress modestly because this is a religious ritual." Aunt Suad was quiet for a moment. Then she said, "Tomorrow, after we are done, I want both of you to go around the room to kiss and thank each woman for helping us with the Lateefeyeh."

I became even more suspicious when my aunt asked us to thank all the women, as if we were the ones who asked them to come. But since Aunt Suad was big on proper behavior and social graces, I dismissed my suspicion.

Aunt Suad was like everyone's grandmother. She was born in 1900, the oldest of her eight siblings and the first child to survive after my grandmother's two miscarriages. While she had only a sixth-grade education, men and women, relatives and friends, including my grandfather, sought her advice. At the same time, she was self-centered and very funny. I recall her yelling, "I'm having a hot flash! I'm having a hot flash! Fan me, fan me!"

Granted, I did not quite understand what that was all about.

They sat on the floor in the muraba'a juwanni, the women's guest room, in a large circle. The room was dark and cold. The wood-burning stove didn't seem to help much. Some of the women placed small blankets on their laps, while others had on sweaters or shawls. All of them wore white prayer headscarves, but no one was praying. They were talking very quietly.

I looked around, wondering what I was supposed to do. I saw Arwa sitting next to Aunt Suad, but there was no room for me to sit next to her. Luckily, Aunt Nahida noticed me. "Come here, sit next to me," she said, patting the carpet as she moved to make room for me. I took off my slippers, tiptoed over quietly and sat on the carpet next to her.

"Let's start with Al-Fateha, the first verse of the Quran," said Rasmyieh Khanum.

We lowered our heads, put our palms facing up on our knees and read a short verse from the Quran. "*Bism Allah al-Rahman al-Raheem*, in the name of God the merciful, amen."

Once done, we all wiped our faces with our palms and sat still, waiting.

Rasmyieh Khanum took a large cloth bag out and dumped its contents on the carpet in front of her. It looked like a pile of large brown beans.

"What does she have?" I whispered in my Aunt Nahida's ear.

"Be quiet," Aunt Suad said. "You can't speak while doing the Lateefeyeh."

"We're ready to start," announced Rasmyieh Khanum. "I'm going to pass these beans around one at a time. As you hold the bean, say 'ya lateef,' and then pass it to the woman next to you. I have one thousand blessed beans here. There are twenty of us. Once we pass all of them around we will be done. Then, we'll read Al-Fateha again." After that she said, "Bism Allah...ya lateef, in the name of God, the kind," and passed one bean to the woman on her right. Then she passed another one, and another one, until the twenty women were saying in unison "ya lateef, ya lateef, ya lateef," while moving their hands to receive and pass the beans. After a while the repetitiveness of 'ya lateef' and the hand movement made me feel light-headed and semi-hypnotized. I also felt euphoric and high.

We sat there for hours doing that. Then Rasmyieh Khanum announced that we were done. It was time to read al-Fateha again.

When I stood up, I felt dizzy. The women were moaning, "Ya Allah, it's so hard to get up." "Give me your hand." "My back is killing me." "My knees are so sore."

"Go tell Fawziyeh we are done. Ask her to bring us water and coffee, and to get dinner ready," said Aunt Suad. The women sat on the diwans lined up against the four walls of the room, rubbing their knees, shoulders and backs.

~

A couple of weeks after the Lateefeyeh, Aunt Suad said, "I have good news for you. Your mother called. The phone lines and the borders are now open. She wants you to come home."

"Thank you, Khalto, thank you! This is the best news. I'm so happy." I hugged and kissed her many times. Then I said, "I miss my parents and Ayman so much. Please Khalto, can I go to Amman tomorrow?"

"Your Aunt Nahida and I will take you and your sisters. We need a couple of days to get ready."

"I can't wait, I can't wait."

Arwa, Susu and I were so happy to go home. None of us liked the school in Damascus. And we missed our parents, brother and friends.

The day we were about to leave, Khalto Suad asked me, "Do you still have that Nasser picture?"

"I do. It's in my bedroom."

"Don't take it with you to Amman. You should leave it here."

"But I want to take it. I want to show it to my parents and friends."

"Didn't you hear me? I said leave it here."

"Why?"

"Because Jordanian security officers are searching people at the borders. They will definitely take it from you. They might not even let you enter Jordan," said Aunt Suad.

I was sad to leave Nasser behind. In my next visit to Damascus, I was unable to find the picture. I accused Aunt Suad of destroying it. Although she denied having anything to do with its disappearance, I never saw that picture again.

Our trip to Amman was uneventful. There weren't many people at the borders. We made it home in less than six hours, which wasn't bad, considering the political situation.

To my surprise, our street was lined with cars on both sides, and our home was so packed with people that we could hear them from the street. "Arwa, what's going on? Why are all these people here?" I asked.

"How would I know? Let's go find out."

I reluctantly walked into our home, holding Suad's hand, while struggling to locate our parents and Ayman. I found my mother in the living room with lots of women, mostly friends, neighbors and my father's relatives. I ran to her. She hugged Susu and me and started to cry.

"Mama, why are you crying?" I asked, ready to cry myself.

"I'm just happy to have you home."

I wanted to ask what all these people were doing at our home, but that would have been considered rude, so instead I asked where Ayman and Baba were.

"Your father is in the guest room. He has visitors too."

"Can I go see him?"

"Sure, go ahead."

"I want to go too," Susu said, and she ran ahead of me.

I stood by the guest room door. I searched for my father among the many faces. Some I knew and others I did not. I was shocked when I saw him. He was so skinny and dark. I hardly recognized him. Suad was already sitting squeezed next to him. Ayman sat on his other side.

"Ayman, Baba." I rushed to them. When I tried to hug Ayman, whom I truly missed, he pushed me away. He was at that age when boys were embarrassed to be hugged in public. Then I embraced and kissed my father. He hugged me back quickly, then let go of me. When I was growing up, men did not display much affection, especially in public. I wanted to ask why he looked so skinny, or why there were so many people in the house. Instead, I quietly left the room. I was so bewildered, trying to wrap my head around the whole ordeal.

"Mama, what's wrong with Baba? Is he sick? Why are all these people here?"

"Your father is not sick. He's just tired, that's all. People are here to congratulate us for his release from al-Jaffer detention center."

I stared at my aunts. "How come you never told me Baba was in jail? You lied to me! How could you hide the truth from us for so long? He's my father, I should have known."

I wasn't just angry. I was traumatized by the fact that my aunts would actually lie.

My mother held me. "Anan, don't be upset and don't talk to your aunts this way."

"How come no one told me that my father was in jail? All this time and I didn't know. Why didn't you tell me? Why? Look at him, he looks so sick." I started to cry.

"He's not sick. He lost some weight, that's all. He'll put it back on in no time. You should be happy your father is finally home and we're all together now."

With all the guests gone, my father gave my sisters and me big hugs and kissed us, saying, "I missed you so much!"

At eight o'clock sharp, as we always did, we sat around the dinner table. My father wanted us to tell him about our school in Damascus and if we had made any friends. We, on the other hand, wanted to hear about jail.

"It wasn't all that bad," he said casually. "The worst part was the first few days when I was held in Amman's jail in a separate cell. No one would tell me why I had been arrested. But once I was taken to al-Jaffer it was okay. To my surprise, many of my friends were there. Anyways, now we're all home, and that's what really matters."

I wanted my father to tell me more, but he said he was tired and wanted to go to bed. "I'll tell you more later," he said as he left the table.

After Baba retreated to his bedroom, my mother and aunts sat in the living room talking until the late hours of the night. They kept asking me to go to bed, but I wanted to hear what they had to say. I was still mad at my aunts for lying to me.

"We're so happy to see him home. Poor sister. These six months must have been really hard. We're happy the girls were with us."

"I'm happy for that, too. Thank you for taking care of them. I'm so glad Ayman stayed with me. I needed him for comfort and company."

"Tell us what happened. How could they arrest Abu Arwa when he held such a high position in the government? How could they get away with arresting the director of the Jordanian Civil Service Department?" asked Aunt Suad.

"Well, this government has no shame or respect for anyone. A few days after the military coup in Iraq, Abu Arwa went to Bahouth bookstore in downtown Amman, where he buys most of his books. While browsing, two members of the secret police walked in the store and arrested him right on the spot. I'm glad his driver, Abdel Hadi, was with him. He came straight home and told me what had happened."

"Why did they arrest him? What do they have against him?" asked Aunt Suad.

"We still don't know. They arrested lots of people. Most of the men in our neighborhood were arrested. Abu Arwa was never charged or questioned. It took me more than a month to know that he was sent to al-Jaffer."

"Mama, where is that?" I asked.

"It is in the desert by the Saudi border. There's nothing there. Prisoners don't try to escape, even if they could. They would die from heat and thirst before anyone could see them."

"But how about all his friends in the government, couldn't they help?" asked Aunt Suad.

"I tried. I called everyone I knew."

"My brother Rashad said he was arrested because he is a communist."

"Abu Arwa isn't a communist. He is a socialist," my mother replied.

"According to Rashad, there is no difference."

"Look Suad," my mother said, angrily. "I love my brother, but when it comes to his politics, he's so reactionary."

Wanting to change the subject, Aunt Suad started telling my mother about the Lateefeyeh. "Wallah ya Siham, we had the Lateefeyeh only two weeks ago, and now Abu Arwa is released. It worked."

"I don't believe in that, but thanks anyway."

Later I asked my mother, "Khalo Rashad doesn't like socialists, but he and Baba like each other, don't they?"

"Of course they do. We're all family, and that's what matters the most."

Within a few days, life went back to normal, except my father had no job. I was happy to go back to my school and be with my friends.

"How come you stayed in Damascus all this time?" asked one of my classmates.

"Her father was in jail. That's why they couldn't come back from Damascus," said another.

"Why was your father in jail?" asked a third girl.

"Because he's a communist," said a fourth one.

"He's a socialist," I said, then added, "I think communists and socialists are the best," not knowing exactly what either was.

A second-grade classmate of my sister Suad told her, "Your father was in jail because he stole tomatoes." Suad cried all night long.

14. Kennedy in Beirut

Beirut, 1963–1964

Mama picked up the phone. I tried to repress my tears as I heard her voice through the scratchy line. I was homesick, but wasn't about to admit it. It had been only a couple of weeks since I left to attend Beirut College for Women, BCW. Like all mothers, Mama could detect my sadness.

"What's up? Are you all right?"

"I'm fine Mama. I just want to know if we are Sunni or Shi'a.[27]

"You mean to tell me you called just to ask this question? What difference does it really make?"

That was a time when making a phone call between Beirut and Amman required calling an international operator, giving her the country, city and phone number, then waiting by the phone to be connected. Sometimes it took over an hour of waiting. International calls were also expensive.

"I have to fill out a form. Mrs. Habeeb didn't believe me when I told her I wasn't sure."

"I don't understand. How does your religion have anything to do with your college education? And who is she, this Mrs. Habeeb?"

"She's the foreign student advisor."

"What a stupid question. We're Sunni."

My mother was not that enthused about me attending this college from which she had graduated twenty years earlier. I wasn't that happy either. During my senior year, Mama kept trying to convince me to go to the University of Jordan.

"It is a good university and many of your friends are going there."

"How come Arwa gets to go to college outside of Jordan? How come she gets to go to the American University in Beirut?"

"Well, maybe that wasn't a good choice. She's having a hard time with all of the classes taught in English. You won't have that problem at the University of Jordan since classes are taught in your own language."

"You can't make me live here," I said.

"You don't have to. You can live at the dorm if you want," said my mother.

"You know what I want. I want to go to Cairo University. That's what I want."

"Cairo is too big and too far. You can go there for your graduate school."

"But Mama, I want to go there now."

As a teenager I was interested in politics. I loved Nasser, Lumumba and Che. Cairo was the cool place to be. It was the center of political activism, and it was also the center of Arab culture—theater, music, film and art.

"I tell you what," my father said. "If you don't want to stay in Amman, you can go to Beirut. It might be too late to apply to the American University, but you can still apply to Beirut College for Women. You'll be in the same city with Arwa."

"But I don't want to go to Beirut. I want to go to Cairo."

"You heard your mother. You can go to Cairo for graduate school. And if you don't move fast sending your application, you might end up staying right here with no college at all," said my father, bringing our argument to a close.

That is how I ended up at the BCW, an American missionary college. I was happy to get away from my parents, but I wasn't that happy to go to an all-women's college. What was the point in going to college if it had no boys?

With my few belongings packed, a couple months of spending money and the tuition check, I was as ready as I could be.

"Do you have your money and passport?" asked my father.

"Yes Baba, I do."

"When you travel, you should always be sure you have them."

"I know. You already told me."

"Let's have our breakfast then and get going."

We sat at the dining table. My mama looked distraught. She was not eating, but had prepared my favorite dish, fattet hummus.

"Thank you, Mama. I want you to tell me how you make it."

"It's easy. You put the toasted pita in the bottom of a deep dish, top it with the cooked chickpeas, add the sauce and then sprinkle the toasted nuts."

"But how do you make the sauce?"

"You mix yogurt, tahini, crushed garlic, lemon juice and salt."

"Yallah, come on, Anan, finish your breakfast. We need to go," my father said, interrupting my cooking lesson.

My father was to drop me downtown at the travel agency that ran taxis between Amman and Beirut. My parents had been arguing over my travel plans all week. As we were about to leave, my mother pleaded again with my father.

"I don't understand! Why can't you drive her to Beirut? She's too young to travel on her own. It's only a few hours' drive. You can take her, see Arwa and come back tomorrow."

"Sooner or later she needs to learn how to travel on her own."

"Mama, I'm not that young. Don't worry about me. I'll be fine."

"Your father is so stubborn. Call me as soon as you get to the college," Mama said with tears in her eyes. "Don't forget to call Arwa. She'll come help you unpack." She hugged me tight, then started to cry.

"Please Mama, don't cry. Arwa will help me if I need anything. I promise I'll call you as soon as I get there," I said, trying not to cry myself.

"*Allah ma'ek ya binti*, may God be with you my daughter. Be good, be careful. Don't forget to call."

When I hugged Susu to say good-bye, she also stared to cry.

"Don't cry," I told her. "You can come and visit Arwa and me. We'll have great fun."

Ayman had left the room as soon as he was done with breakfast. My mother had to call him.

"Ayman, come here. Come say good-bye to your sister."

Without much enthusiasm he did come and gave a quick hug. Probably he was relieved to see me go. Poor Ayman, I never really gave him much attention, and I did favor Susu and took her side whenever they got into an argument or fight.

My father and I got to the downtown taxi station a few minutes before nine. The station owner was sitting behind his desk, smoking and sipping coffee while reading the newspaper. As soon as we entered his office, he got up and came from around his desk to shake my father's hand.

"Good morning, Abu Arwa."

"Good morning, Abu Riyad. This is my daughter Anan. She's the one traveling. Which car will she be taking?"

"That one." He pointed to a large American car. It looked almost new.

"Who's the driver?"

"Abu Ahmed. He's standing right there, next to the car."

"Is he leaving on time?" my father asked.

"Yes, as soon as he finishes his coffee. All the passengers are here."

My father walked over to the taxi driver. "Al salam alaykum, may peace be upon you, Abu Ahmed."

"Wa alaykum al salam."

"This is my daughter, Anan. She has never traveled on her own. She's going to Beirut College for Women. Do you know where that is?"

"I do. I take students there all the time."

"Here is an extra half-dinar. Can you please take her all the way to the college?"

"Inshallah, I'll do that as soon as I drop the rest of the passengers by Beirut's taxi station."

When it was time to leave, my baba hugged me tight. His teary eyes, which he tried to hide, made me so sad. I wasn't used to seeing Baba cry.

~

I arrived safely at my dorm, and as instructed I called Arwa as soon as I got there. She arrived within thirty minutes to help me unpack.

"Mama gave me money to buy new clothes. Would you come with me?"

"I'd love to. I know all the fashionable stores. Beirut is really modern, not like Amman."

Arwa, who had a flair for fashion since childhood, went with me and we bought all that I needed. Since we had to wear uniforms for school, I did buy a lot. For the first time, Arwa acted like the older sister. She not only helped me pick out my new clothes and shoes, but she also took me to nice restaurants on the Mediterranean Roche and to hip cafes on al-Hamra Street. And when I had my first date with a Syrian guy from her university, she took me to get my hair done and then dressed me up. I didn't like the guy and never went out with him again. As it turned out, he was my first and only date during my time at BCW.

I was happy to have my sister there. Before coming to American University, Arwa had left home when she was only sixteen to attend a boarding school in the West Bank city of Nablus. For the last three years, I saw her only on short vacations. I think she hated coming home, and she always managed to find a way to take summer classes. For the first time, our sibling rivalry seemed to subside, although I was still envious of her looks. Arwa grew up to be a stunningly beautiful young woman, and many of the male students wanted to go out with her. She had many dates, and often she would come to borrow a sweater or a jacket, which I never saw again. Thankfully, I was smaller and most of my clothes didn't fit her.

To my surprise, and in spite of my desire to go to Cairo, it didn't take much to fall in love with Beirut, which was a more cosmopolitan city than Amman. True, I had been to Lebanon numerous times before, but never on my own. I relished the freedom of being away from my parents. I even liked the very tiny dorm room I shared with Nadia, a Libyan from Tripoli, who was, like myself, a freshman. Most importantly, I was delighted to have Che Guevara take center stage in my room. "Good morning my friend. Good morning Che" were the first few words I uttered in the morning as I looked at his large poster.

"You're crazy," Nadia would say.

"Look at him. He's so handsome, isn't he?"

"That's why you have his poster. It has nothing to do with his politics."

"That's not true," I insisted. But I have to admit, his looks did make it easier to be so enamored with him.

Before long, Nadia and I became best friends. Neither one of us was very fond of the college, especially when it came to its politics, religion and strict rules.

"I don't understand why we have to attend chapel every morning. They don't expect us to convert, do they?" said Nadia as we were sitting in our room chatting.

"I don't understand it either. I hate being told over and over again how Jesus Christ saved us from our sins. Why do they think we have sins? I'm also tired of hearing how great the United States is. They think they're better than us!"

"I agree. I don't like hearing that either," said Nadia.

"It seems like nothing has changed since my mother graduated from here. Maybe we can ask Mrs. Habeeb to allow us to skip chapel."

"You must be crazy. What makes you think she'll listen to you? I'm not going. I'm scared of that woman," said Nadia.

"Well, I never prayed at home, let alone went to a worship house everyday. I hate having religion shoved down my throat."

"Anan, I don't think talking to Mrs. Habeeb is a good idea," advised Nadia.

It didn't take me long to realize that Nadia was right. Going to Mrs. Habeeb was, in fact, a terrible idea.

"I'm told you wanted to see me," said Mrs. Habeeb.

"Yes, Mrs. Habeeb."

"And what is this about?" She was still looking at her desk. Our eyes never met.

"I want to ask your permission not to go to chapel," I said while trying to stop my voice from cracking.

"What? Not to go to chapel!"

"But I'm not Christian, and we never practiced any religion at home."

"That's the problem with your parents. They didn't even bother to teach you if you are Sunni or Shi'a."

I felt a sharp pain in my throat and tried to hide my tears. *Don't cry Anan, don't let her see your tears,* I said to myself.

"Mrs. Habeeb, please don't speak badly about my parents."

"You're not going to tell me what to say, are you?"

"No, Mrs. Habeeb, I'm not. But I would like you to tell me how you would feel if someone made you go to a mosque everyday?"

The minute these words escaped my mouth, I knew I would pay heavily for them.

"You are a rude girl. Maybe you don't belong in this college. I want you to leave my office right now."

Within a couple of days I received my first disciplinary notice.

A month or so later, while studying in my room, I got a call from the guest dorm receptionist.

"Anan, there is a woman here who wants to see you."

"Who is she?"

"Her name is Mrs. Hassa. She said she's a friend of your parents."

I rushed to my dorm's guest lounge. I was so excited to have Auntie Hikmat visit me. I hadn't had any visitors since I arrived, except for my sister Arwa.

The day after, I was called to Mrs. Habeeb's office.

"Sit down, Anan."

I did as ordered. Honestly, I didn't like this woman at all. I don't think she liked me, either. She had never said a nice word to me, or smiled, since I had arrived.

"You know why you're here?"

"No, Mrs. Habeeb, I don't."

"You know that you're not allowed to wear pants in the guest lounge, don't you?"

"When did I do that?"

"When that so-called friend of your mother's came to visit you."

"You're right, Mrs. Habeeb. I'm really sorry. I was so excited I didn't even realize I was wearing pants."

"Do you know the rules of this college? No respectable woman wears pants in public. We are trying to teach you how to dress like a classy lady. Only skirts and dresses are allowed, and they cannot be too short. Do you understand?"

"Yes, Mrs. Habeeb, I do. I just forgot to change."

"Do I have to write you a second disciplinary as a reminder?"

"No, Mrs. Habeeb. This won't happen again. I promise."

By November, I had made a few friends and wanted to have a birthday party at the dorm. Before I invited any of my friends, I was sure to check with the dorm supervisor. I was not ready for a second disciplinary notice. I was delighted when I got permission to hold the party in the dorm's second-floor lounge. The approval came with a laundry list of what I could or could not do: no loud noises, no loud music, no dirty jokes, no liquor, clean the lounge after, all outside guests have to sign in, and absolutely no boys.

On the morning of my birthday, I woke up with a start as I heard the emergency loudspeaker announcement.

"Attention, attention. All classes are canceled. Mrs. Habeeb wants all of you to be at chapel by seven-thirty."

I looked at my watch. It was already seven.

"What's going on?" I asked Nadia as she sat in her bed rubbing her eyes.

"How would I know? Let's go find out."

As we settled in our seats at the chapel, Mrs. Habeeb addressed the crowd, saying, "This is a very tragic day for us and for the world. President John F. Kennedy was assassinated yesterday. The college will be closed for three days. We will be having a memorial service here at ten o'clock sharp. You should put on appropriate clothes. Black is preferable. If you don't have black, then wear something dark. No makeup. The president of the college will be here. You'd better be on time."

Mrs. Habeeb rushed out before we had a chance to ask any questions.

As we left the chapel, students gathered in the dormitory lounge discussing the event. When did it happen? Who killed him? And why?

"Why should we close the college because an American president is killed? You think schools in the US would close if Gamal Abdel Nasser were assassinated?" I asked the gathering students.

"This is an American college, that's why," answered one student.

"But this is an Arab country. This is not America," said another.

Within minutes, students were involved in a heated discussion, arguing passionately about Kennedy and Nasser, about colonialism, imperialism and national independence.

"Oh my God, it's almost ten," yelled one of the girls.

We rushed to our rooms, washed our faces, combed our hair, changed to darker clothes and ran to the chapel.

That afternoon, as I was decorating the lounge for my birthday party, I was called to Mrs. Habeeb's office. For a second, I thought she wanted to wish me a happy birthday, but that was too good to be true.

I entered her office and stood by the door.

"Sit down," ordered Mrs. Habeeb, pointing to a chair by her desk.

I did as I was told. Mrs. Habeeb was not a particularly attractive woman, and all students feared her a great deal. With her mourning outfit and no makeup, she looked even more terrifying. I could tell she was upset. I wondered if I had anything to do with it.

"Anan, you better listen to me carefully because I mean every word I'm going to say. If you plan to stay at this college you had better show some respect."

Totally taken by surprise, I asked, "Mrs. Habeeb, what did I do now?"

"How could you say that we shouldn't cancel classes when such a tragic event happened?"

"Mrs. Habeeb, this is tragic for the Americans, but why is it tragic for us? Besides, I was only trying to understand why we should close for three days. I didn't say we should or shouldn't."

"Don't try to be too smart. I won't allow it. I also heard you didn't cancel your birthday party. Is that true?"

"Mrs. Habeeb, I don't understand. Why should I?"

"There's not going to be any birthday party. Do you understand me? We're done. You can leave now." Her voice was getting louder.

"Fine, Mrs. Habeeb, I will cancel the party. But no one has answered my question. Why should we close our college if an American president is killed?"

"You are hopeless. Just leave. Do you hear me? I want you to leave right now." She was shaking and I was getting really scared.

I left. I canceled the party, and even restrained from participating in any further discussion about Kennedy's assassination. I still received a second disciplinary note.

For the remainder of the school year, I struggled to stay out of trouble. A third disciplinary notice would have meant my expulsion. By June, I packed my belongings and my Che Guevara poster, and said farewell to my friends. My unpleasant experience at the college did not taint my love for Beirut. I knew I would miss the Mediterranean beach terribly, the great restaurants, the cultural life, the city's vibrancy and all that this great city had to offer. And I knew, one way or another, I would be back.

At Beirut College for Women in 1963, with classmate Sana Darwazeh (right).

In my Che Guevara T-shirt, around 1973.

15. THE WONDERFUL SIXTIES

Amman, 1964

I carried my few belongings to the curb waiting for the taxi to take me and four other students home. I looked back with mixed emotions, wondering if I would regret my decision not to return to Beirut. The picture-perfect BCW campus, with its lush trees, flowering bushes and grand buildings, was rather alluring. It was the reality behind this seductive beauty that made me want to escape.

We started our six-hour journey at ten o'clock in the morning. I sat in the backseat, drifting off into my own world and reflecting on my one-year experience. I was totally oblivious to the other students, talking and laughing as they revisited their adventures with men, love and lust, ignoring the disapproving looks of the driver.

"What's wrong, Anan? Why are you so quiet?" my friend Sana asked.

"I feel a bit sad leaving Beirut, but not this stupid college."

"What do you mean? Aren't you coming back?"

"No, I'm not. And I haven't told my parents yet. They're going to be really mad."

I had been anxious about my parents' reaction since I made my decision a few months earlier. I was planning to write, but I kept putting it off, trying to find a way to soften the blow. For my parents, college education was not a choice; neither was Cairo University, where I intended to go.

As soon as I settled in at home, I told my parents, "I'm not going back to Beirut. I hate the college. That is why I didn't do well. I shouldn't have gone there in the first place. I'm going to Cairo University, and I'm going to major in political science."

With the speed of a bullet, I spelled it all out. I didn't want to think or worry about it anymore.

To my surprise, my parents were not as upset as I anticipated. They didn't scream, or say "How dare you!" Their reaction, or lack thereof, alarmed me. *This is too good to be true,* I told myself. *I wonder what they have in store for me?*

A couple of weeks later, I brought up my plans to go to Cairo University.

"It's too late to get accepted for the upcoming school year," my father said.

"No it's not. Not if I go to Cairo right now and submit my application in person."

After many arguments, and begging and crying, my mother convinced my father to let me go. She bought me a plane ticket, gave me some money and off I went to the city I had been longing for.

Cairo was much bigger than I anticipated. It was crowded, hot and dusty, but it had its own charm. The Nile, the Pyramids, King Tut's jewelry, the opera house, the movie theaters and the live performances were overwhelmingly thrilling. And, of course, the gigantic Tahrir Square surrounded by so many wide avenues. I still recall how I thought I had accidentally joined a demonstration when a massive number of people rushed to cross the square adjacent to Tal'at Harb Street.

Eager to be the first to the registrar's office to submit my application, I took a taxi at seven-thirty in the morning and rushed to the university. I was sure that being there early and in person would improve my chances for getting accepted.

"When will I know?" I asked as I handed over my application.

"We have lots of foreign student applications. We have to finalize the Egyptians first," said the man at the registrar office.

"When will you do that?"

"I'm not sure."

With its free and reputable universities, Egypt attracted a large number of Arab and African students. I was worried that I might not be accepted.

"How many foreign students do you have? Will you give priority to students from Arab countries?" I asked.

"Don't worry, each country has its quota. The number of applicants from other countries will not affect your chances."

"Are there many from Jordan?"

"I don't know. Why don't you come back in a week. Inshallah, we'll know by then."

As told, I came back a week later.

"Have you finalized the foreign student applications?" I asked.

"Not yet. Come back next week."

The following week I went back, only to get the same answer.

"When will you know?" I begged. "I love Cairo, I love Egypt, I love Nasser and I want to go to this university."

I was hoping my expression of intense love would improve my chances.

"*Ya ukhti,* sister, we love you too. Inshallah, you will be accepted. We should know by the end of the week. Come back Thursday."

A few Thursdays passed, the school year had already started and my parents were losing their patience. One day my father called and said in a very firm voice, "We got you accepted to the University of Jordan. Come back. You can't just keep wandering the streets of Cairo."

"I don't want to come back. I hate Amman. I don't want to live at home," I cried back.

Of course, without my parents' financial support, I couldn't stay. I carried my broken heart and eyes filled with tears back home.

The next four years, I lived at home and attended the recently established University of Jordan. It was the first in Jordan and had the promise of high educational standards.

The University of Jordan, a free public institution, was very different from Beirut College for Women. Its students, especially the males, came from humble backgrounds. UJ was their only hope to get a college education. The female students, however, mostly came from the middle and upper-middle class; their families preferred to have them stay home rather than study abroad. The class disparity between the two sexes kept them apart, especially when it came to romance.

For me, having students from working-class backgrounds was a plus, since they tended to be more political and radical than the women. Soon I became friends with several who shared my leftist idealism, and even flirted with a few. UJ was my first experience with a coed school, and I liked it. With my dark skin and skinny body, I had grown up thinking I wasn't that attractive. But having male students telling me how beautiful I was and chasing me felt really good. It even made me a bit cocky. Little did I know they would have said the same things to any woman who gave them the time of the day.

One day I agreed with Hisham, who had been flirting with me for a while, to meet at the British Council to watch a movie. I took Susu with me, which I often did. When Hisham held my hand after the lights went off, my heartbeat hit the roof and my throat got so dry I couldn't grasp what was happening to me. Later, when my father found about it, he told me in a very firm voice, "Don't you ever take your sister with you." I had no idea how he found out about it and was totally shocked that he didn't say more, like "I don't want you to ever go out with boys."

Initially, I resented attending the University of Jordan and resented my parents for forcing me to go there. But that worked to my advantage. My parents, feeling a bit guilty, let me come and go as I pleased—until my mother found out about my love life. Many of my friends from high school were there, and I made many new lifelong friends. The political activism on campus suited my radical tendencies. It didn't take me long to enjoy being in Amman and at university, but for the life of me, I wouldn't admit it to my parents.

Interestingly enough, I never heard from Cairo University as to whether I was accepted or not. I adjusted quickly to life at the University of Jordan, and I didn't seem to think much about it. But it later dawned on me that Cairo University must have written back with the outcome of my application, and my parents didn't tell me. My guess is that I was accepted. Seeing me finally settled and content, my parents decided to keep the information to themselves, not wanting to rock the boat.

The University of Jordan was only three years old. It had a total of four hundred fifty students, and only liberal arts with limited majors. Classes were small, which allowed us to establish friendly relationships with classmates, as well as professors. When I graduated in 1968, the total number of our sociology department graduates was only eleven. The university, however, did not have a political science major, which I wanted to study.

"You can major in sociology, it's the closest to political science. You can major in that in graduate school," Baba said.

"I want to work when I graduate. I don't want to go to graduate school."

"You're not going to find a good job with only a BA, whether in sociology or political science," my mother insisted.

For a change, I listened to Baba's advice and majored in sociology, with a minor in philosophy. I enjoyed liberal arts much more than science, which had been my plan at Beirut College for Women.

The best part of being at UJ was getting involved in all of the political protests and organizing, which alarmed my parents, especially my father. Having himself experienced the Jordanian regime wavering between liberal and oppressive, and being jailed for his own political convictions, Baba wanted to protect me.

"You need to finish your college degree first. Then you can make your own decisions about your political involvement."

"But I'm not young. I can't just sit back and watch other students being involved."

"I know this Jordanian regime very well. Look at me. Today I'm the Minister of Foreign Affairs; tomorrow I might not have a job, or may even be in jail again."

"Why do you work with the Jordanian government then?"

"If all the liberal and progressive people refuse to take part, we would have a more oppressive government."

My parents' advice not to get too involved went in one ear and out the other. These were probably the most exciting and liberal years in Jordan's history. Stores and street vendors were loaded with books, magazines and political posters, ranging from Marx and Lenin, socialism and communism, and world revolutions to Lumumba, Malcolm X, Che and Castro. Hardly a month went by without me joining a demonstration, or sit-in, or signing a petition. Along with thousands of others, we rallied for women's and workers' rights, for democracy and a free press, for Arab unity and, of course, for a free Palestine. These were my formative years, the years I experienced many firsts, including a first love and a first job. These were also the years when my father and I, despite our many conflicts and disagreements, created a very special bond. Most importantly, these were the years when I developed my political and social consciousness. Just like the rebellious 1960s in the US, these were our sixties, when we learned about international solidarity and demanded a more just and equitable world. And I was thrilled to be in the midst of it all.

16. First Job, First Love

Amman, 1965

During my sophomore year, I met Hani Snober, a young man who had recently returned from Europe with a degree in theater. With youthful idealism and fervor, Hani set his goal to establish Al-Masrah al-Urduni, the first professional theater in Jordan.

"Look at all these beautiful posters," I told my friend Huda. "There are going to be live performances for the whole month of March, each week one play. We should go."

"I've never been to a professional theater before. I hope they're better than the ones we used to do in school," she replied.

"Of course they are. I saw a few when I was in Egypt. They were awesome."

"But they're expensive. The cheapest ticket is a dinar," Huda said.

"I don't care. It's worth it. I'm going to all of them."

The first season, held at the university, had four politically and socially charged plays, reflecting the mood of the 1960s. The auditorium was packed with an enthusiastic crowd, clapping and cheering. The acting, the clothes and the stage décor were all mesmerizing. After each performance, I would stand in line, along with many admirers, wanting to meet this Hani Snober and the performers.

After attending the first season, I kept fantasizing about being an actress. I kept telling my friend Huda, "Wouldn't it be cool if we became actresses?"

"Are you serious? My parents would disown me."

One evening, Huda came over to our home holding a newspaper.

"Anan, did you see today's paper? The Jordanian Theater is looking for actresses."

"Let me see it."

I grabbed the newspaper from her hand and, sure enough, there was an ad with a date and time for auditions.

That evening, while we were having dinner, I declared to my parents my decision to become an actress at the Jordanian Theater. My mother stared at me, perplexed.

"An actress in theater?"

"There's an audition this Thursday afternoon. I want to go."

"You need to focus on your school. Theater will only take you away from studying."

"I won't let it affect my grades. I promise."

"You have no experience in theater or acting. I hate to see you rejected."

"Don't worry about me. I can handle it."

I couldn't contain my excitement when I got a call from Hani Snober telling me I was accepted. After a few sessions of training and reading scripts, I got a major role in one of the plays. It was a Spanish story about a rebellion of fishermen in a small village against a large corporation that was destroying their livelihood. With my radical politics, the role and the subject were just what I was looking for. The second season had five plays and lasted over one month. Like the first season, all the performances addressed political and social issues. We had a larger and more enthusiastic crowd.

Before we started preparing for our third season, Hani Snober called all the theater members for an emergency meeting.

"I have some good news. You aren't going to believe this."

Being a theater professional, he paused for a few seconds to up the suspense.

"Yallah ya Hani. Spit it out!" we begged him.

"Anyone want to guess?"

"No, just say it," the stage manager insisted.

"Well, today I met with the Minister of Culture, upon his request. He said that the ministry wants to adopt us as the official theater of the Hashemite Kingdom of Jordan. They will provide us with a practice space, pay our expenses and every one of us will receive a monthly stipend."

"I don't believe it," said one actor. "Since when does our government care about art and culture?"

"You must be kidding," said another.

"How much money are we talking about?" yelled a third.

The twenty of us were all talking at the same time, cautiously excited, not sure if we were to believe what we had just heard.

A month later, after that meeting, I received my first monthly salary: fifteen dinars. That was good money for an amateur actor in college. At the time, the monthly salary of a schoolteacher with a college degree was only thirty dinars.

"Look, the Ministry of Culture is paying me fifteen dinars a month just to act. I must be very good," I told my parents. I even started dreaming about a career in theater. Thank God I didn't know much about Broadway, or I would've been heading there.

Little did we know, that was the government's way of coopting us. By the time we started selecting the plays for the third season, our director Hani Snober was summoned to the Minister of Culture and was told that he must first submit copies of all the plays for the season to the ministry for approval. For good or bad, my acting career came to an abrupt halt. I was not about to sell my soul for fifteen dinars.

~

At the Jordanian Theater, I found my first love, Jawad. A tall attractive man in charge of the stage décor, he was eight years older than I was, divorced and had three kids. He was poor and didn't have much college education. Being a Christian did not add to his charm, in my parents' eyes.

I kept my relationship a secret from my parents. We all did. But Amman was no more than a large village where you couldn't hide much. Before long, my mother found out and had a fit. She would list all his unbearable qualities.

"You're too young to understand. He's using you. If you don't stop seeing him, I'll tell your father and let him handle you."

Of course, I kept seeing him. I was twenty-one and so much in love. And who listens to their parents at that age? I treasured the attention I was getting—to have a man open the car door for me, take me to restaurants and bars, introduce me to cigarettes and gin and tonics. He made me feel beautiful, desired and sophisticated. Whether it was love or lust, I was totally infatuated. My mother was getting more and more upset. She kept threatening to tell my father. I got so tired of her threats, I decided to tell him myself.

Talking about love and boyfriends was not a conversation I'd ever had with either of my parents. Not having a clue about how my father would react, I took the seat closest to the door in case I needed to flee. My hands were shaking. I spilled most of my Turkish coffee in the saucer.

"Baba, I want to tell you something," my voice trembled.

"What is it?" he asked, alarmed.

"Please don't get mad at me. I met this guy at the Jordanian Theater and I like him…"

After I finished telling my father about the love of my life (omitting information I knew he wouldn't like), Baba sat motionless, deep in thought, eyes focused on his lap for what seemed like forever.

My chest tightened and my tongue searched for saliva. His silence was frightening. I didn't know what to expect. Finally, he said with as much calm as if he were giving a lecture about love, "It's normal at your age to feel attracted to a man. However, you shouldn't think of marriage now. You're very young and you have to finish your education first, and I don't mean just your BA." He paused, then added, "And you should exercise regularly."

"You're not mad at me? You mean I can see him?"

I couldn't understand what exercise had to do with love but decided to leave it alone. It wasn't until years later that I realized that my father thought exercising might reduce my sexual appetite.

"I don't want you to go out with him alone, but you can go with other friends," my father advised.

I was trying to comprehend the enormity of what had just happened, but Baba interrupted my thoughts. "Keep this conversation between us. You don't need to tell your mother about it."

I was so shocked by how cool he was that I didn't even ask why he didn't want me to tell Mama.

One day my mother saw me with my boyfriend walking down the street. As soon as I entered the house, she was waiting, furious, to say the least. Actually she was trembling and so pale I thought she was about to faint.

"What kind of a daughter did I raise? Walking with him in daylight right by our home. What are the neighbors, the shopkeepers, and our friends going to say? You're giving me an ulcer, or a heart attack! You're damaging your reputation and the *suma'a* of your sisters and our family. We are respected people, and now our reputation is ruined."

She was so mad and went on and on about how my love was damaging her health, the family reputation, and how she was unable to face her friends and her *akaber*, classy, Jabri family. At that point, I lost it too and started screaming as well.

"You don't like him because he's Christian. You say people's religion doesn't matter. You don't even fast or pray, so what if he's not Muslim?"

"It's not about his religion. He's older. He's divorced. He has kids and he has no education. Can't you see that? Can't you understand? Our family's reputation is at stake."

"What reputation? Two of your brothers died young from too much drinking, and your brother Rashad, whom you're so proud of, is a womanizer, having affairs. Don't tell me I'm the one damaging your family reputation."

Mother started crying.

"You're not my daughter. I don't want to ever talk to you again."

I felt really bad, but being a stubborn twenty-one-year-old, I was not about to apologize. To add insult to injury, when she threatened to tell my father, I said, "Go ahead, I already told him."

My father was furious. He could understand his twenty-one-year-old daughter being irrational about her love choices. But to talk to my mother in this fashion was crossing a line. When he called me to his office and asked me to close the door, I knew I was in big trouble.

"Don't you ever talk to your mother that way. And don't you ever talk to her about her family."

"But what I said was true."

"Your mother isn't responsible for what her brothers do."

"But she told me I'm damaging the family's reputation."

"Listen, I'm not interested in your smart responses. You will go right now and apologize to your mother, and don't ever be disrespectful to her again."

Before I reached the door he said, "You better understand, you're not going to get married to anyone before you finish your college education. And I don't just mean your BA. I mean at least your master's."

I did apologize to my mother, and like all mothers, she forgave me for what I said, but never for having that relationship.

As my father had hoped, by the time I got to graduate school, I was no longer in love. My father was socially liberal, and we were allowed to do what most of our friends couldn't. But he had absolutely no tolerance for abusive language. Even the most common words kids use when fighting or arguing—like 'stupid,' 'fatso,' 'ugly' or even 'hey you'—were off-limits. Jawad, on the other hand was neither that liberal, nor that polite. He was extremely jealous and would get angry if my dress was too short or if I went out with male friends—things that my parents had no issues with. Initially I interpreted his jealousy as love and his harsh words as "he's just upset." I kept telling myself *once he knows how much I love him he'll change.* But the longer we were together, the more he thought he had the right to tell me what I could or couldn't do. Finally, I came to realize how stifling his love was, and to experience how too much love could actually suffocate me.

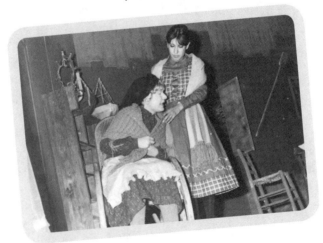

Anan (*right*), with the Jordanian Theater, in Amman, 1966.

17. Es Samu Village

I had already been dismissed from high school twice. The first time was for leaving school to join a demonstration, when the principal gave us clear instructions not to. I was suspended for only three days. My parents didn't seem to be that upset. That was during tenth grade.

The second time was during my junior year, when the principal uncovered that, along with two other students, I was plotting to run away to France. She locked us in her office and called our parents, insisting they come and get us in person.

"Please Mrs. Husseini, don't call our parents. We promise we'll go directly home," I begged.

"You're going to stay here until one of your parents comes. I don't trust you."

My father and I sat in the principal's office as she reported the problem at hand.

"Please forgive them, they're young and don't know what they're doing. Anan, go ahead and apologize to Mrs. Husseini," instructed my father.

"I am sorry, Mrs. Husseini. I won't do this again."

"I don't blame you for being upset. I'll be sure to discipline her as soon as we get home."

While driving home my father started his interrogation.

"Why do you want to run away to France? How were you planning to support yourself? Where were you going to sleep, eat and go to school?"

"Well, I can work and go to college there."

"Tell me the truth, how did you come up with this idea, and how long have you been thinking about it?"

My friend Muna, who ultimately became a famous artist, wanted to go to Paris to study art. Coming from a rather conservative family, she didn't think her parents would approve of her choice, so she decided to run away. As she shared her plans with me and another friend, we got very excited about the adventure. We had been reading French literature and were enamored with Jean Paul Sartre, Simone de Beauvoir and Albert Camus, although I'm not sure how much we comprehended their feminist and existentialist theories. But the prospect of being in France felt exhilarating. Getting ready for our adventure, I started saving my meager allowance and began hiding food cans for the trip. I even remembered to pack a can opener.

"Anan, I just asked you whose idea it was. Answer me." My father's voice interrupted my reflection on our failed plan.

"The three of us came up with the idea. We had been thinking about it for a couple of months."

"Let me tell you something. You don't need to run away. You can go to college in France, but first you have to graduate with good grades and learn some French. However, I want to make it clear that I won't tolerate it if you get in trouble at school again. You understand?"

"Yes, Baba, I do."

Amman, 1966

As if I wasn't in enough trouble with my parents over my love affairs and political activism, the Israelis had to make it worse. On November 13, 1966, they attacked Es Samu Village in the West Bank, which was under Jordanian control, killing sixteen, injuring more than fifty civilians and demolishing forty homes. People in Jordan took to the streets protesting the Jordanian government's inability to stop the attack. The protest spread fast, and students at the University of Jordan walked out of classes and occupied the campus. The Jordanian army came in and arrested a large number of male students. Thanks to sexism, no female students were arrested, but six were kicked out of school, including myself.

In truth, I wasn't that upset at being kicked out of the university. On the contrary, I felt proud. It was a badge of honor that added to my popularity among students, but I was terrified of my parents' reaction.

When the university demonstrations took place, my father asked me if I had anything to do with them.

"No Baba, I just stood there and watched."

"Are you sure?"

"Yes, of course I am."

Two days later, I was summoned to the office of the university's president.

"The army has your name as one of the organizers. They have an order to arrest you. I asked them to leave your punishment to me. You'll be permanently dismissed from the university."

"Please, Dr. Assad. You can't do that. My father is going to be furious."

"You should have thought about that earlier."

I went home terrified but didn't utter a word, hoping that, by some miracle, my parents would never find out. But I couldn't help imagining and rehearsing my confrontation with them. Three days later, my father came home from work and said he wanted to talk to me.

"Anan. How many times do I have to tell you? You can't keep getting kicked out of schools and universities."

"What was I supposed to do? Just sit there and watch the demonstrating students?"

"You have to finish your education first. Being out of university isn't an option. Do you understand?"

"I'm almost twenty-two. I can make my own decisions."

"Listen to me. From now on, and as long as you live in this house, you'll do what I tell you. I don't care how old you are."

"Well, I don't have to live here. I'm leaving."

I ran out into the street, went to our bedroom window and called my sister. "Susu, Susu! Baba kicked me out. Get me some money from Mama's purse. Here, take my slippers and hand me my shoes. Hurry up."

We were never allowed to look in my mother's purse. But Suad managed to get me some money and my shoes. Unlike Ayman, Susu and I continued to be close throughout our lives. During her childhood, I took care of her and treated her like my own daughter. By the time she became a teenager, I began sharing all my 'secrets' with her. Trust me, between my love life and political activism, I had a lot of secrets. On the other hand, my relationship with Ayman was distant but civil. We managed to coexist without dealing much with each other. Our politics were a world apart. He supported the Hashemite monarchy and loved King Hussein. And when he wanted to aggravate me, he would call Nasser names and theatrically imitate the way I talked about political and social issues. I have to admit, Ayman had the greatest sense of humor. He made me laugh really hard, even when he was making fun of me and of my choices. To this day, whenever Ayman and I talk over the phone, he tries to provoke me by mentioning some political or social issues I'm passionate about. Then he starts making fun of me, and we both laugh across the wires that connect Jordan and the US.

I put on the shoes Suad handed me and stuck the money in my pocket, still trying to figure out what to do next. I wasn't at all upset. On the contrary, I felt liberated. I recall standing in the street inhaling and thinking, *Freedom at last, freedom at last!*

My friend Najwa, who was also a student at the university was already married and living in the city of Irbid, a one-hour drive north of Amman. I decided to stay with her until I figured out what to do next. Whatever that was, I was not going back to my parents. But my excitement about my freedom was short-lived. Najwa had not shared the information about my dismissal with her husband. With the university being closed and the continuing political unrest, he didn't suspect much. But he kept asking Najwa why I was staying with them. Meanwhile, I was getting restless. There wasn't much to do in Irbid, and most importantly, I was away from the love of my life. So when my Aunt Naima called, suggesting I go home, I was relieved but didn't want to admit it.

"I'm not going back. He kicked me out."

"My dear Anan, if you stay any longer at Najwa's, her husband might kick you out as well."

"But I'm not going back to his house."

"He is your father. He loves you."

"No. I told you. I'm not going back."

After arguing back and forth, my aunt, trying to talk some

sense into my head, and me, being a stubborn twenty-one-year-old, my aunt finally said, "Anan, habibti, you can't stay at Najwa's forever. Come back to Amman. You don't have to go home. You can stay with me."

Aunt Naima's daughter, Nihal, was also one of those kicked out of the university, but her mother didn't seem to be as upset as my father. I agreed to go stay at my aunt's, knowing that I couldn't stay there for long. Nihal and I were very close, and I loved my aunt and her family. They tried their best to make me comfortable, but with a small three-room house and eight kids, there wasn't much room for an additional person.

One afternoon, after being at her home for a few days, Aunt Naima said, "I visited your parents today. They want you to come home."

"But he kicked me out."

"Your father was upset. He didn't mean it."

With no job and no money, I didn't have many choices. Also, I missed our home and my family. Together, my Aunt Naima and I walked the quarter-mile to my parents' house. Since we were about to have a serious talk, we sat in the guest room. Only my father was home. We sat there in silence for what felt like ages.

Finally, Aunt Naima said, "Anan is sorry. She wants to come back home."

I was furious by what she said. To keep from further aggravating the situation, I kept quiet.

"I'm very concerned that she will never get a university degree," my father said. Then he turned to me and said, "If you want to be independent, you have to have a decent job, and that doesn't come without a university degree. There's no women's independence without economic independence. It's as simple as that. Do you understand?"

"Yes I do," was all I could say.

A couple of days later, my father came to my bedroom and handed me a newspaper clipping.

"Here, you need to read this."

It was a part of a speech by Fidel Castro addressing Havana University students: "The best way you can serve Cuba and protect its revolution is by being good students." This was before Google.

I had no clue how he was able to produce that article just in time. Luckily, the university let us back after one month, and peace temporarily returned to our home.

To my parents, going to college was a given and not an option.

"In our world, your brother—or any other man—can make his living selling tomatoes on the street corner, and that wouldn't be *eib*, wouldn't be shameful. As a woman, what will you do if you don't have a college degree?"

My mother repeatedly said this to my sisters and me. Of course, with three daughters and only one son, she was just as determined that he would never be selling tomatoes, or any other vegetables, but would be getting a good education, as well.

Although I returned home, I never lost the desire to get away from my parents. Between my bad choice in the love department and my political activism, my parents were keeping a closer eye on me. The prospect of not finishing my college education, or getting married to Jawad, tormented them. Before the end of my junior year, and with the help of our professor, Dr. Seri Nasser, my friend Muna De and I managed to get an interview for a summer internship at the Bethlehem Mental Health Hospital.

"I'll put in a good word for you with the director of the hospital, but you have to go there for an interview," Dr. Nasser said.

The internship included room and board in the female staff wing of the hospital. After the interviews, the director took Muna De and me on a facility tour, treated us to lunch at a nice restaurant, then drove us to the taxi station. As we said our goodbyes, we shook hands, with the understanding that we would be back in three weeks at the end of the school year.

As soon as he drove away, Muna De and I started jumping up and down like kids.

"We got it, we got it! That was easy. Dr. Nasser made it sound much more complicated."

"Tomorrow we'll go out and celebrate," Muna De said.

"I'm celebrating being away from home."

"You're right," said Muna De. "Even if that means spending our summer vacation at a mental hospital."

But the Israelis wouldn't leave us alone. Only a week after our trip to Bethlehem, the June 6, 1967, war erupted, and within days, the Gaza Strip, East Jerusalem and the West Bank—including Bethlehem—fell under Israeli occupation. Overnight we were banned from going there. The University of Jordan closed, and our final exams were postponed to the beginning of the following school year. Many students from the Palestinian Occupied Territories were cut off from their families. And we wore the shame of our humiliating defeat for many years to come.

Instead of interning in Bethlehem, I ended up volunteering at one of the newly constructed camps helping Palestinian refugees settle in to their new homelessness. Most had been living in refugee camps in the West Bank since 1948. The Israelis did not trust having them live in their new territorial acquisition. From their perspective, would it really matter if they were made refugees once or twice?

18. AMNEH

Baqa'a Refugee Camp, Jordan, 1967

She was young, bright and poor. She knew life only in refugee camps, and she hated it. She was born in A'qabat Jaber, a refugee camp in Jericho that hosted thousands of Palestinians who were forced out of their homes in 1948. In 1967, all of the residents of A'qabat Jaber were forced to move to Jordan. Twelve-year-old Amneh, along with her parents and four siblings, found refuge in the Baqa'a camp, hastily constructed on the outskirts of Amman to host the new flood of Palestinian refugees.

In 1962, fourteen years after the Nakba, while still living in A'qabat Jaber, Abu Ahmed, Amneh's father, received the letter he had been waiting for. His heart pounded as he carefully opened it. "*Shukran ya* Mustafa, thank you! Um Ahmed, look what we got. Mustafa kept his promise. He's sending us money from Kuwait. We'll be able to buy the farmland."

"*Al Hamdu laka ya Allah*, thank you God," said his wife Aisha. "Inshallah, soon we can move out of here. Fourteen years is more than enough."

"*Saber ya*, Um Ahmed, be patient. It's going to take me time to buy the land and plant trees. But I'll start with growing vegetables to give us some income while waiting for the trees to produce."

"Wallah, you deserve this, Abu Ahmed. You've been working so hard since we came here. I want to see our kids living outside this camp, getting an education and, inshallah, going to college. Especially Amneh, she's a bright girl."

"Allah kareem," said Abu Ahmed.

Within five years, and before he had a chance to move out of the camp, Abu Ahmed lost his new farm to the Israelis in the aftermath of 1967 war. For the second time in his life, he had become a refugee.

"I hate life here. I look all day but can't find work. Everyone else is looking. How are we going to eat?"

"Allah kareem ya Abu Ahmed. *He* doesn't forget *His* people."

"It looks like *He* does."

"Saber ya Abu Ahmed, saber, be patient. We're just like thousands of others."

"I'm done standing in line for UNRWA rations. Wallah, if it weren't for you and the kids... "

"Don't talk this way Abu Ahmed."

"I'm standing in line since 1948, when I was eighteen. My father refused to stand in the UNRWA line. Since I was the oldest, I had to. Now I'm thirty-five, with my own family, and I'm standing in line again. Who else is going to? You?...Amneh, a twelve-year-old girl?"

"I know it's hard, wallah. But what else we can do?"

A few days after the 1967 war, I told my friend Leila, "I'm so ashamed by our defeat. I feel so sad about the loss of the rest of Palestine, especially Jerusalem."

"Me too."

"We can't just sit idle. We must do something, but I don't know what."

"UNRWA is looking for volunteers at the new Baqa'a refugee camp. It's only a few miles north of our university," said Leila.

"But I wanted to do something more than helping refugees."

"Like what?" Leila asked.

"I don't know. I get crazy ideas some times. But I suppose helping refugees is better than doing nothing. I bet you Muna and Samiha will join."

"Let's first go there and find out what kind of volunteers they need."

In the hot, desert-like and crowded Baqa'a camp, we allocated tents, distributed food, clothes and blankets. We reported missing children, parents, wives and husbands. After a month of extreme chaos and confusion, and feeling all the energy of the young people, Leila said, "We should set up a special tent and start teaching these."

"That's a great idea," said Samiha, who loved to sing. "I'm dying to teach them some uplifting songs."

In the school tent, I taught reading, writing and arithmetic. Leila told stories with happy endings. Samiha taught hopeful songs about returning to Palestine, and Muna taught the kids to draw.

"It's therapeutic. It'll help them deal with the war and cope with their losses," said Muna, who bought paper, paint and coloring pens. She spent hours with the children, and they talked, cried and drew.

The children drew planes and tanks and bombs. They drew destroyed homes and dead bodies. They talked about their crying mothers, angry fathers and dead loved ones. They wrote letters to God, asking why? Out of that came Muna's book, *Children in Times of War.* Among these children was Amneh, Abu Ahmed's older daughter.

Amneh loved reading, writing and painting. She drew pictures about the war and wrote prose and poems about going to college, having another life and getting away from the camp. "It's hot, it's crowded. Adults are always screaming and yelling."

In her senior year, Amneh talked more and more about her dream of going to college. Her father's response was always, "Inshallah."

"You promised. You've been telling me to study hard and get good grades so I can go to college."

"I didn't think we would be in this camp forever. I thought we would go back to Jericho, to the farm your uncle helped us buy."

"But Baba, that's not my fault. I know you can't pay for my education. I will manage on my own. I'll work. I'll get a scholarship."

"I said inshallah."

"You're the one who told me over and over 'you might lose your home, your land, your country, but no one can take away your education.' Why did you keep saying that if I can't go to college?"

"Who knows what will happen by the time you finish school? Who knows if we will be alive?" was his answer.

"But this is my last year of school. I'll be done by June."

"Stop nagging me! Leave me alone."

Every few weeks, Amneh again would bring up the idea of going to college and argue with her father until he would lose his temper. Her mother felt caught between the two of them, not knowing whom to comfort first. Often Um Ahmed would plead with them both to stop arguing. "Leave your father alone, he's tired. He has enough to worry about." To her husband she would say, "Please take it easy on the poor girl. She's a good child."

After living in the Baqa'a camp for years, Abu Ahmed's resignation had gone beyond despair. He had given up on finding work. But he couldn't bring himself to share his thoughts with anyone, not even his wife.

Amneh, the oldest and the brightest of his kids, was about to finish school, and she became his only hope.

Beirut, 1973

When Amneh graduated from high school in 1973, both Muna and I had left Jordan and were living in Beirut, where the Palestinian revolution had found refuge after its 1970 bloody confrontation with the Jordanian army. For young activists, Beirut was the place to be.

One morning, Muna came to visit me in my apartment, which I shared with my sister Suad. She had with her a copy of *Children in Times of War*. As we sat on the balcony drinking coffee, Muna opened the book and said, "You see this picture?"

"What about it?"

"Do you remember Amneh, the smart girl at the Baqa'a camp?" Muna asked.

"Vaguely."

"Amneh, the girl who drew this beautiful picture, has finished high school. She wants to come to Beirut and go to college."

"That's great. Good for her." I commented.

"But she needs our help," said Muna.

I looked more closely at the picture. I couldn't understand what was so beautiful about a child's drawing of airplanes dropping bombs. But I assumed that was not the point.

"We'll help her. But what exactly does she need?" I asked.

"Amneh has no place to stay. And she has no money. As you know, my place is very small. Can she stay with you?"

"Ahlan wa sahlan, I'd love to help her," I said.

"She's coming against her father's will. She's been accepted to al-Arabiyeh University, but she can't afford the tuition. We need to help her find a job, get a scholarship and find a room at the dorm."

Filled with enthusiasm and a sense of adventure, I said, "No problem. We can do it."

Amneh's six-hour journey from Amman to Beirut went relatively smoothly. Muna and I met her at the taxi station around four in the afternoon. It was hot and humid. Amneh's old but very clean summer dress stuck to her tiny body. Her unruly curly hair framed her smooth bronze face. She looked disoriented and tired.

I carried her small, raggedy bag, and we took a taxi to my apartment in al-Hamra, a trendy neighborhood.

"Here is your room. It's small but hopefully it will do," I said, as I placed her bag by the bed.

"*My* room? I never slept in a room by myself. It's bigger than the room I share with my four siblings."

"You must be starving," I said.

"I am. But can I wash up first and have a nap? I am very tired." She sounded on the verge of crying.

"Are you all right?" I asked.

"Yes, I am…I'm just tired."

That evening we celebrated Amneh's freedom by going out to dinner, then to a movie. As we returned to the apartment, Amneh started crying. I wasn't quite sure how to comfort her. After all, we were strangers. She could hardly remember me, and she had never before met my sister Suad.

"I didn't tell my parents about my plan to come here. I'm so worried about what my father is going to do when he finds out. Poor Mother, I'm sure he'll blame her for my escape. That's why I didn't tell her. After he went to work, I left them a letter and told my mother I was going to visit a friend."

"Don't worry, your father will be mad for a few days, then he'll get over it," I told her as I gave her a hug.

A few days later, while having breakfast, Amneh asked my sister and me, "Do you remember the first day I was here, how much I cried?"

"I sure do."

"That was the scariest day of my life. I not only didn't tell my parents about my plans, but it was my first day away from them. It was also the first time I traveled, other than our trip from one refugee camp to another. I had never crossed borders before or been in an elevator, to a movie or to a restaurant."

My God, I thought to myself, *how much I just take for granted.*

"Sorry, I should've thought about it. I hope we didn't overwhelm you."

"It was scary, but it was also exciting," said Amneh. She had a big smile.

I couldn't help but be amazed by this one-hundred-pound remarkable young woman, who was totally oblivious to her intelligence and beauty. Amneh was able to adapt to her new life very quickly. Within days, she learned how to use public transportation and to go from my apartment to al-Arabiyeh University. She was happy to be away from her depressed mother, angry father and crowded dwelling. But she kept wondering about her family, especially her father. I kept assuring her that "Everything was going to be just fine."

Amneh stayed with my sister and me for a month and then moved to the dorm. I would call her daily to be sure she was okay.

"I'm fine, wallah I'm fine. I just love it here."

A few days after she moved, she came to visit me at my apartment. Muna came by to see her.

"Yesterday I sent my parents a letter apologizing for leaving without telling them. Now that I'm settled, I want them to know where I am and how I'm doing."

"I'm glad you did that," I said.

"I was reluctant, but I love my mother and father. I spent hours writing the letter until I finally got it the way I wanted it. I think it's a very good letter, and I'm proud of myself."

"If I remember, you loved to write. I'm sure it's a good letter," I said.

"Maybe I should have let you read it first. I told them all about you and Muna, and how much you two helped me. I just don't want my father to be mad at me," Amneh said as she frowned, bringing her thick brows together over her piercing black eyes.

"Once he knows that you're already enrolled in college and have a scholarship and a job, he wont be mad anymore," Muna said.

"You think so?"

"Trust me, parents don't stay mad at their kids for long," I said.

"I told him about the scholarship and my plan to live really frugally and send him some money. I also told him, once I graduate I'll get a good job and help my brothers and sisters go to college."

"You're amazing. Your parents must be very proud of you," I said.

Amneh's dreams about freedom and a brighter future didn't last long. One evening only a few weeks after writing to her father, he arrived at the dorm. He was threatening to kill her and kill those who had helped her run away.

"Where are those whores? Where do they live? Take me to them."

Amneh screamed as he grabbed her by her long hair.

"No one helped me. I did it on my own."

"You liar. You told me about them in your letter. You're a whore, just like them."

Amneh ran into her room and locked her door. It took the dorm supervisor and two faculty members to convince her father that Amneh was a wonderful student. But all their pleading to let her stay was to no avail. But he promised to take her home, not hurt her and leave Muna and me alone.

Amneh packed her few belongings and her dreams of a better life and accompanied her father back to the Baqa'a camp.

Muna stayed in touch with her. As he promised, Amneh's father didn't punish her for what she did. Soon she found a job.

Later, she managed to graduate from the University of Jordan.

19. A Shirt and a Tie

Damascus and Amman, 1971

I arrived at the outdoor taxi station in downtown Damascus just before ten in the morning. The station was muddy, congested and noisy. Drivers were calling out their destinations, trying to lure passengers: Amman, Irbid, Beirut, Aleppo, Tripoli. Children, mostly boys, were announcing their merchandise: chewing gum, cola, candies, Kleenex, cigarettes. Young men carrying small trays with cups of coffee and tea were squeezing between people and cars calling, "*Kahwa, chai…kahwa, chai…*coffee, tea." Women sat on low wooden chairs with their baskets of fruit and vegetables, of which there wasn't much, since the winter season was already approaching. And there was the bread man, calling "*Taza ya ka'ek, taza,* fresh sesame bread," selling his sesame-covered bread, zaatar and boiled eggs. Although I'd had breakfast only an hour ago, I couldn't resist the temptation of the fresh ka'ek, so I bought some.

Within seconds, I found myself surrounded by half a dozen young boys.

"Let me carry your bag. Let me help you," they offered.

"Thank you. I don't need help."

"You don't have to pay me. Just let me carry your bag."

"I don't need help with my bag. How about if I buy some chewing gum from you."

"How about candies?" asked another kid.

"Buy some Kleenex. Please, buy some," said a third one. They pushed each other while yelling, "Please, buy from me. Buy from me."

I tried my best to distribute my leftover Syrian money among them. I put my purchase in my bag and walked away, searching for a car to take me home. The distance between Damascus and Amman is only a hundred seventy-six kilometers, but the trip could take between four to eight hours. It all depended on the traffic, the weather, the mood of the customs officers and, most importantly, the relationship between the Syrian and Jordanian governments, which was not particularly good at that time. It was early winter 1971, a few months after the bloody confrontation between the Palestine Liberation Organization and the Jordanian army. Syria verbally sided with the PLO.

"Amman, Amman! Only one seat left," yelled one of the drivers.

"Going to Amman?" I asked.

"Inshallah," he said. "God willing, we'll be leaving soon."

"Where's your car?" I asked.

"Right there," he said, pointing to a yellow Mercedes.

"You said you have only one seat left. I see only one passenger in your car."

"The others went to buy something to drink. They'll be back in a minute."

The car, from the 1950s, appeared to be on its last leg. I wasn't sure it would make it to Amman. Realizing my reluctance, the driver grabbed my small bag and threw it in the trunk.

"Have a seat," he said, "we'll be leaving soon."

As I opened the door to the backseat, the driver said, "Would you please sit in the front. The backseats are taken."

"Taken by whom?"

"By other passengers. They should be here any minute."

An old man was sitting in the front seat. He moved painfully to the center to make room for me. After ten minutes of waiting, I opened the door and got out of the car.

"Where're you going?" asked the driver.

"You keep telling me they're coming soon, but I don't see anyone. I'm sorry. I need to find another car."

"They have to come back. Their bags are in my trunk."

"They better come back soon. Otherwise I have to find another car."

"Be patient ya binti," said the old man. Then he turned to the driver and said, "These kids! They have no patience."

"I'm losing my patience, too," the driver shot back. "I'm half tempted to leave their bags on the curb and look for other passengers. With all the tension between Syria and Jordan, business has been very slow. So many delays at the borders. Most days I can do only one trip."

"Allah yefrejha, may God ease the situation," said the old man.

The driver, middle-aged, possibly in his late forties, looked tired. He patiently stood by his car, waiting for the other passengers.

"Can I buy you some coffee or tea?" the driver asked us, as a young man with his tray passed by.

"No thanks," said the old man, and so did I.

The driver bought a cup of tea and was standing by the car sipping it when the three passengers, accompanied by two young men, came back. It was almost eleven.

"Where have you been? My other passengers have been waiting. Come on, get in and let's get going," said the driver interrupting their conversation, as they stood near the car chatting with their friends.

The three male passengers were fashionably dressed. I could smell their strong cologne. They were students at the University of Damascus going home for a visit. Once we left the noisy station and hit the main road to Amman, the driver looked in his mirror at the students.

"What kind of travel documents do you have?"

"Jordanian passports," answered one of them.

"All of you?"

"Yes," said the three in unison.

The driver had already asked the old man and myself the same question. We also had Jordanian passports.

"That's good," said the driver.

"Why? Don't you like to have Syrian passengers?" I asked.

"Well, it all depends on which direction I'm traveling. If I'm entering Jordan, having Jordanian passengers means less hassle on the Jordanian border. When I come back to Syria, having Syrian passengers is easier."

The driver then turned to the old man and asked, "Do you have any merchandise?"

"Just a couple boxes of candy and some toys for my grandchildren."

The old man couldn't have had much. His clothes were patched together and their color was fading. His face was carved with deep lines and his hands were rough.

"How about you?"

"I don't have much, just my clothes," I answered. The driver then looked into his rearview mirror and addressed the young men in the backseat, "Do you have any merchandise?"

"We have nothing," said one of them, irritated to have their conversation interrupted.

"How about books or any subversive literature?"

"We told you we have nothing," said another.

"I don't like asking my passengers all these questions, but I have to. They're searching every car at the Jordanian border. I'm just trying to save my customers and myself trouble. That's all."

"Don't worry, son. Everything, inshallah, is going to be all right," said the old man.

The aging Mercedes was shaking and making strange noises as the driver picked up speed. "Slow down my son, slow down," said the old man.

"What's the matter with you? Are you scared of speed?" asked one of the backseat passengers. Then he added, "Don't listen to him. We want to get home before dark."

"Don't worry, we will be slowed down at the border," said the driver, changing the radio to a news station.

"Don't change the radio. Who wants to listen to the news?" complained one of the students.

By then, the attitude of these young men was getting to me, but I bit my tongue. I guess that's the price to pay for sharing a taxi with strangers. The driver, ignoring their request to change the station, kept listening to the news, which soon caught my attention. *"Heavy fighting erupted this morning in the northern Ghor between the PLO and the Jordanian Army. The fighting continues until this hour. Talks about ceasefires have collapsed,"* announced the news reporter.

"Allah yosturha, God help us,*"* said the old man.

"That's our life, always delayed," said the driver. Let's just hope the road to Amman isn't closed."

As we arrived in the Syrian border city of Dar'a, the driver asked us to give him our travel documents and follow him to passport control. The old man had a hard time getting out of the car. To our delight, leaving Syria was rather quick. We were hoping to have the same luck with the Jordanians.

At the border city of Ramtha, less than a mile from Dar'a, the driver asked the three young passengers and me to follow him.

"You can stay in the car. If they ask for you, I'll come and get you," said the driver addressing the old man.

"Shukran ya ibni, thank you, son."

At passport control, the officer was looking at travel documents and calling out names of passengers. After examining one passport closely, he asked, "Are you Fadi Sahawneh?" pointing to one of the students.

I got a bit nervous, and the driver looked concerned, as well. We were worried the Jordanian would decide to interrogate or even arrest him.

"Yes, that's me," answered the student.

"How are you related to Abu Najeeb Sahawneh?"

"He's my uncle, my father's brother."

"Oh my God. He is my best friend. Please give him my *salamaat*. Tell him Abu Ziad at the border sends his greetings."

"I will."

"Also tell the customs officer that Abu Ziad says hello."

We zipped through customs as quickly as we did through passport control. The car and our luggage were hardly searched. That's the blessing, and curse, of living in a small country. One can always count on running into someone who knows your family, your neighbors or your friends.

"Are we done?" asked the old man.

"Yes, we are. Thanks to the Sahawnehs. Let's hope the rest of our trip will be as quick and easy," said the driver.

After we had driven about twenty-five kilometers from the border, we started to see and smell the fighting smoke over the Ajloun Mountains. The driver turned on the radio. The news reported heavier fighting. Soon we were stopped by an army checkpoint.

"Where are you going?" asked one officer.

"To Amman," said the driver.

"Where did you come from?"

"Damascus."

"Open the trunk," ordered the officer.

The driver did as he was told.

As we started driving again, the old man asked the driver, "Are you all right ya ibni?"

"This is our life. I don't know how we can support our families when we can only do one trip a day and endure all of this."

"Saber ya ibni, saber, you just have to be patient," said the old man.

We encountered another checkpoint on the outskirts of the Baqa'a refugee camp, housing thousands of Palestinian refugees from the 1967 Arab-Israeli war. After the officer asked the driver where we came from and where we were heading, and after checking our passports and luggage, we started off again. By then everyone was quiet, including the three young men in the backseat.

"What's that?" asked the old man, interrupting our anxious silence. He was pointing to a huge satellite dish opposite the Baqa'a camp. The contrast between the poverty of the camp and the newly constructed dish was hard to miss.

"It's a satellite," echoed the three back passengers in unison.

"What's a satellite?" asked the old man.

The three in the back seat competed to answer. "It cost fifty million Jordanian dinars to build," said one of the men.

"But what is it?"

"It's for television. Now we can watch live events, like the Olympics," said another one.

The old man started laughing. He laughed so hard that tears ran down his face. Everyone was looking at him, curious to know what was so funny.

"Why are you laughing?" asked one of the young men, sounding upset.

"Nothing," said the old man. "It's nothing." He wiped his eyes with his sleeves, but then added, "It's like buying a fancy tie when you don't even have a shirt."

20. More Trouble on the Way

Amman, Cairo and Beirut, 1968–1973

"Now that you're a bit older, you can attend any graduate school you want," said my mother.

"But I don't want to go to graduate school. I want to work, to save some money, to get my own place…"

"You can't support yourself with a BA in sociology."

"Let me work for two or three years, then I'll look into it."

"I'm afraid once you start working, you won't go back to school."

And so went the discussion for most of my senior year. With all the political excitement happening in Amman, and between my numerous activist friends, and most impor-tantly, still being madly in love with Jawad, I wasn't interested in leaving. My father, totally ignoring my lack of interest, was applying on my behalf to the American University of Beirut and to universities in England.

"But Baba, I'm not ready for graduate school."

"We lose nothing by applying. You might change your mind once accepted."

Since I wasn't the one doing all the tedious work of filling out applications, I let it be.

The summer I graduated from the University of Jordan, my father was appointed

My graduation from the University of Jordan in 1968.

the Ambassador of Jordan to Egypt. As much as I wanted to stay in Amman, that was my opportunity finally to live in Cairo. "Now you can fulfill your dream of going to Cairo University," said my father.

"Isn't it too late to apply? And what if I don't get accepted?"

"You have good grades. You will."

Only my sister Suad, who was in her senior year of high school, and I accompanied my parents. My sister Arwa was at AUB getting her master's, and my brother Ayman was on his way to a university in England. As a courtesy offered to diplomats, and despite our late applications, I was able to enroll at Cairo University, and Suad was enrolled in a private high school.

It didn't take much for me to become enchanted with life in Cairo. While the university campus lacked the intense political activism I left behind, cosmopolitan Cairo was overwhelmingly thrilling. I was particularly enamored by the Khan al-Khalili historic souq, the politically progressive theater and by Cairo's Opera House, where I was first introduced to performers from around the world.

Only six months after we arrived in Cairo, my father's appointment ended abruptly.

"I should have known better. One can never trust this government. They're claiming I met with the Soviet delegation, which was visiting Cairo last month, without consulting the State Department."

"That's strange," my mother said. "I thought you did consult with them."

"Of course, I did. I gave them ample time to respond to my request. But I never heard back, so I just went. They're pretending they never received my letter. I know they did."

I felt badly for my father to lose his job in this humiliating fashion, and for my mother who was as much in love with Cairo as I was. At the same time, I was delighted to finally live on my own. My sister Suad and I remained in Cairo until the end of the school year. Suad continued on to AUB to study architecture, while I went back to Amman to do my field research for my master's thesis. My friend Muna De, who had graduated with me from the University of Jordan, was already working at the Jordanian television station. I often shared with her my desire to find a good-paying job that would allow me to break away from my parents.

"There's an opening for a program director at the station. Why don't you apply?"

"Thank you for telling me. I'm so eager to earn some money and find my own place."

"Do you really think your parents are going to let you live on your own?"

"Why not? They want me to be independent," I insisted.

"Don't kid yourself. How many young women do you know live on their own in Amman?"

"How come men do?"

"Only if they find a job in another city. As women, we're doomed to stay at home until we get married…or maybe die," she said, laughing.

"I don't think I will."

Working at the Jordanian television station was a treat. The salary was good. Even better were the working hours, from four in the afternoon to midnight, which made my parents accustomed to me staying out late. But the Israelis, who managed endlessly to mess with our lives, wouldn't leave us alone. They started bombing different locations in Jordan under the pretense that they housed Palestinian fighters who were launching attacks on Israel, or intending to.

Anan (*third from right*) working at Jordanian Television, in 1970.

"Baba, please help me understand. Why are the Israelis bombing civilians? You should see the footage we have, it's so gruesome, but we aren't allowed to air it."

"The Israelis are trying to pressure the government to get rid of the PLO presence in Jordan."

"But the PLO has so much mass support. Will our government give in to Israeli pressure and push them out?"

"Sadly enough, they might. Besides, the Jordanian government is starting to feel threatened by the PLO's rising popularity."

"You're telling me the Israelis will keep bombing us until they get what they want?"

"I'm afraid they will. I'm also worried about a military confrontation between the Jordanian army and the PLO," said my father.

Sure enough, by mid-September 1970, the tension between the PLO and the Jordanian government spiraled into full-scale urban warfare, which became known as Black September. After two weeks of heavy fighting, Egyptian President Gamal Abdel Nasser called for an emergency summoning of Arab heads of state to end the conflict. On September 27, a cease-fire agreement was reached.

But the strain of the summit was more than Nasser's deteriorating health could handle. He died on September 28 from a severe heart attack, shortly after bidding farewell to Arab leaders. Nasser's death shook the Arab world. Millions flooded the streets mourning his death.

My father (*left*) with Gamal Abdel Nasser, Cairo, 1969.

"Mama, Mama, did you hear the news? Nasser died," I said, sobbing while carrying my transistor radio to the living room where she sat.

"That can't be true. When did that happen?

"Radio Cairo just announced it. He died from a heart attack."

For the next twenty-four hours, I sat in my bed drowning in my own flood of tears, while listening to my radio, hoping that the news reporter would tell us, "*We are sorry. That was a mistake. Nasser is still alive and well.*"

The negotiated cease-fire that killed Nasser was short-lived. By 1971, after multiple armed confrontations, the Jordanian government managed to completely expel the PLO. Defeated and exhausted, the PLO moved its operations to Lebanon.

During Black September, many of us were unable to make it to work. As soon as the fighting subsided, my friend and colleague Ali called.

"Anan, you should report back to work as soon as you can."

"How are things at the station?" I asked.

"You'll find out when you come."

I was totally shocked to see Jordanian army tanks surrounding the TV compound, while soldiers with large machine guns roamed the grounds and the station. Every week, a few staff were fired or arrested, and replaced by regime loyalists. Jordan's temporary openness came to an end.

I took a leave of absence from my work and went back to Cairo to write my thesis. Cairo was gloomy and sad. Apprehension about what the future might bring engulfed the country. I had no desire to do much, either. I left the city as soon as I defended my thesis in January 1971.

In Amman, I came back to my job at the television station, only to find an unbearable work environment.

"All our programs have been censored," said Ali, who insisted we meet at a café. "I didn't want to talk at the station. Most of the new hires are *mukabarat*. They're government spies. I'm going to resign as soon as I find another job."

"The mukabarat doesn't need to hire spies. I heard they already have their own offices at the station," I argued.

Although I was very careful, I was called for questioning more than once.

"It looks like they're after you. I hope you'll not get arrested," said Ali.

"Why would they arrest me? I've done nothing."

"What does that matter? If I were you, I would be more careful."

Ali was right. The atmosphere at the TV station, as well as in the whole country, was rather oppressive. It was the McCarthy era, Jordanian-style.

"I feel suffocated. I can't say what I think, or trust my colleagues, especially the new hires. I want to resign," I told my parents as we were having dinner.

"You never fail to surprise me," said my mother.

"I can't stand being there anymore."

"Be patient. This won't last forever. You have a good job, and with your master's degree I'm sure you'll be promoted soon."

"I can't keep my mouth shut seeing what's going on. Sooner or later I'll say the wrong thing and get fired or even arrested."

"I thought you couldn't wait to get a full-time job. If you resign now, I'm not sure what other job you'll find." She looked at my father, seeking his support. "Abu Arwa, what do you think?"

"I have had my share of bad experiences with this government. It can't be trusted."

"It's your life, you do what you're comfortable with," said my mother.

~

After I submitted my resignation, I went to Beirut and applied for a job at the Palestine Research Center. Meanwhile, my parents used my resignation as an opportunity to start nagging again: "Don't you want to get your PhD? You can get a job as a university professor!"

"No. I don't."

"Look at your sister, Arwa. She is doing her PhD in the States. Write to her, she can help you."

"No," I said firmly. "I'm moving to Lebanon. I've already applied for a job at the Palestine Research Center."

"When did you do that?" my mother asked.

"When I went to Beirut to visit Suad."

"Applying for a job doesn't mean you got one."

"You don't want me to get the job. You want me to stay at home with you and Baba forever. "

"I just want you to wait until you actually have a job!"

"Mama, how many times have you told me 'get that cardboard, that university certificate, then you're free to do what you want?'

What happened to 'Put one foot in the East and one in the West, and I won't ask what you're doing or where you're going'?"

"Your mother just wants you to get your PhD. I don't understand why that is so upsetting to you," my father said.

My parents hardly agreed on much, except when it came to their daughters' education, as if that was their calling. "You have to be financially independent. What if you never get married? What if your husband dies? What if you're unhappily married? Do you want to be stuck for the rest of your life?" And what if this, and what if that? As if we were doomed to disasters that only education could save us from.

After some negotiations, I went to Beirut with their blessings and some of their cash. I stayed with my cousin Aida, and within a month I got the job at the Palestine Research Center.

Aida's apartment was in the Dowar al-Cola neighborhood, not far from where the PLO had settled most of its offices.

On the night of April 9, 1973, I was awakened by a loud explosion that shook our building. I literally fell out of my bed.

"Aida...Aida, I don't know what's going on. Did you hear the explosion?"

Aida and I stood on the veranda trying to figure out what was happening. Within minutes, we heard another deafening explosion. We held each other and ducked to the floor.

"I wonder what's going on?" Aida whispered.

"I wish I knew," I whispered back.

Slowly we stood up, only to see a huge fire not far from our building. A heavy smoke blanketed Beirut's sky on what was supposed to be a beautiful spring night. Minutes later we saw cars speeding down the streets. We tried calling our friends to find out what was going on, but our phone was disconnected.

As it turned out, that was the Israeli's "Operation Spring Youth," which attacked Palestinians in Sidon and Beirut. Three top PLO leaders were killed in their homes in front of their families. A leader's wife, along with scores of neighbors and guards, were also killed. Many PLO buildings were turned into piles of rubble.

The following day, my parents called me at work. "We heard the news. We were able to reach Suad, she's fine, but your home phone is disconnected. Are you all right?" my mother asked.

"It was scary as hell, but now I'm fine."

"You want to come here for a few days?"

"No, don't worry about me. I'll be okay."

"Well maybe you ought to move out of that neighborhood. It's too close to the PLO offices."

"I can't believe my luck. I escaped the horror of Israeli attacks in Jordan and Black September to come to this?" I said, trying my best not to cry.

"You know, you're always welcome to come back home."

"I know, Mama. I know."

Soon after the Israeli attack, I moved with my sister Suad to an apartment in the more fashionable Hamra neighborhood, close to both Suad's university and my job at the Palestine Research Center.

Beirut was Cairo's intellectual and cultural rival. Many Arab writers and artists had come to Beirut to enjoy its political and cultural vibrancy. With the PLO settling in Lebanon, Beirut also became the center of Palestinian activism, attracting many revolutionaries from around the world. The Palestine Research Center, where I worked, attracted progressive Arab researchers and scholars, including the legendary Palestinian poet Mahmoud Darwish and Lebanese novelist Elias Khoury. Among the people who worked at the Research Center was Said Jawad, an Iraqi leftist who had fled the horrors of Saddam Hussein's regime.

One day, Said asked me if I would be willing to host a meeting at my apartment for a Kurdish activist who was visiting Lebanon.

"You have a more spacious apartment than most. I would really appreciate it if you'd open your place for us."

"Of course I will. *Beeti beetac*, my home is your home. But who is he?"

"His name is Jalal Talabani. He's a friend of mine, very progressive, you'll like him."

We sat cramped in my apartment's living room, attentively listening to our guest talking about the plight of the Iraqi Kurds. "All we strive for is to preserve our heritage, to gain some autonomy, to have some control over our lives." Little did we know that thirty-two years later, this tired, shabbily dressed man would become the president of Iraq.

Two years after working at the Center, I decided to make a quick surprise visit to my parents.

"Baba, I brought you a very special gift."

"Don't waste your money, I don't need a thing."

"I bet you're going to love this one."

I handed him a nicely wrapped packet. He turned it over in his hands trying to figure what it was.

"Go ahead, open it."

"It looks like a book," he said, tearing open the wrapping. He carefully examined the book's cover, then read aloud, "*Agricultural and Industrial Growth in Palestine: 1900–1970*, by Anan Ameri." He looked at me, his eyes twinkling with excitement. He kissed the book, then got up from his chair and placed a gentle kiss on my forehead.

"You never told me about this."

"I wanted to surprise you."

"What a wonderful surprise. I'm so proud of you."

Being in Beirut and working at the Research Center provided me with unique opportunities that helped me in my political and intellectual growth, but my meager salary didn't provide me with much. I could hardly make ends meet without an occasional infusion of cash from my parents. To get my actual independence, I decided to take an additional job as a freelance journalist with the Orient Press. After submitting a few articles, the owner said, "Our readers like interviews with famous people. That's what I want you to do."

"Do you have certain people in mind?" I asked.

"No. You have to find them. I'll pay you five hundred Lebanese lira for each interview."

That was twice as much as he was paying me per article. To my distress, however, the only halfway famous people I knew were within the PLO ranks, whose pictures and interviews already saturated the press.

I left the Orient Press office wondering where could I find these famous people. My artist friend Kamal Boullata, who, unfortunately, was not that famous at the time, was living temporarily in Beirut. As we sat in a street café sipping espresso, I shared my dilemma with him.

"The owner of the Orient Press wants me to interview famous people. Where am I going to find them?"

A few days later, I got a call from Kamal suggesting I interview a friend of his who was visiting from the US.

"Who is he?" I asked. "How famous? I never heard of him."

"He's a rising star within the Arab American progressive community."

"Tell me more," I said.

"He is a young activist attorney."

That didn't seem so glamorous. But being desperate for cash I agreed to interview him.

The rest is history. It was love at first sight. That week, I never made it to work. It was April and everything was blooming in Lebanon, including me. A month later, I met him in Paris. I flew to Detroit in July, and in November of that year, 1974, we were married. I have lived in the US ever since.[28]

In September 1982, Israeli troops stormed the Palestine Research Center. They ransacked its interior and stole its entire library, consisting of over twenty-five thousand works. The center's archive about Palestinian history was one of the largest in the world. In February 1983, an Israeli car bomb totally destroyed the center, killing eighteen and injuring one hundred fifteen.

IV

21. You're Either With Us or Against Us

Amman, 1978

My father died on December 15, 1978, a few days short of his seventy-first birthday. His lifelong obsession with a healthy lifestyle, including daily exercise, did not save him from having a severe heart attack that killed him instantly. He died peacefully in his sleep in a hotel room in Prague while attending a writer's conference of the non-aligned countries.

My father, the president of the Jordanian Writers Union, planned to go to the conference via the Amman airport, the logical way to go, since he lived there. To his surprise, the Jordanian security at the airport would not allow him to board his plane. That didn't make much sense to my father. After all, he had a Jordanian diplomatic passport and had held many high government positions, including Minister of Foreign Affairs. Additionally, Jordan had full diplomatic relations with Czechoslovakia and had never imposed a travel ban to that country. But Jordan was also an ally to the West, and the West considered "non-aligned" no more than code for anti-Western and pro-communist. Mind you, some of the founding members of the Non-Aligned Movement, like the Egyptian leader Gamal Abdel Nasser, were in fact anti-communist, but they were also against Western dominance. I guess the logic of "you're either with us or against us" has been US policy, and that of US allies, all along. And Jordan was, and continues to be, a very loyal ally.

My socialist father happened to believe in his individual freedom and in his right to travel to wherever he wanted, whether his government supported such an idea or not. After being banned from boarding his plane, he went home, got in his car and drove a hundred seventy-six kilometers north to Damascus. There, he bought himself a new plane ticket, parked his car at my aunt's home and off he went to Prague.

Upon my father's sudden death, the Czechoslovakians immediately notified the Jordanian government. But since the Jordanian government was mad at my father for defying their orders, they decided not to tell my mother. As she was sitting in her living room sipping Turkish coffee and listening to Um Khalthoum's latest song, three of her closest friends arrived unannounced. The minute they saw my mother wearing a colorful sweater and listening to music, they knew she did not know.

Mama was initially happy by their surprise visit, but she was taken aback once she noticed that the three of them were dressed in black. She realized that someone had just died, but she didn't know who.

As it turned out, Ne'mat, one of my mother's closest friends, heard about my father's death on the local news. She put on her black dress, called her sister Lama'a and told her she would pick her up in a few minutes. They stopped by Juliet's home, picked her up and the three of them came to comfort my mother, assuming she already knew.

Once my mother calmed down from her shock, Ne'mat got the phone numbers of my mother's family in Damascus and of my brother, sisters, and me, scattered around the globe. Arwa was living in Kuwait, Ayman in Beirut, and Suad and I were living in the US in Ann Arbor and Detroit. Poor Aunt Ne'mat, she had the nasty job of delivering the bad news. After comforting me on the phone she said, "Habibti Anan, can you tell your sister Suad? I have so many more calls to make."

"I will," were the only two words I could utter. I sat at the kitchen table next to the phone, not knowing how I was going to tell my sister. I felt totally numb. My eyes, mouth and throat were so dry. I wanted to cry, but I had no tears. I wanted to scream but had no voice. I kept repeating in my head, *Baba is dead...Baba is dead*, unable to imagine my world without him.

The day before I learned about my father's death, I had received a letter from him telling me how beautiful Prague was and how much he was enjoying the conference. His letter was still on the kitchen table. I grabbed it and read it again and again, wondering how he could be gone. To avoid dealing with Baba's death, I decided to delay my arrival in Amman until after the burial. I begged my sister Suad to also wait for a few days so we could travel together. Luckily, she had just met an extremely handsome Colombian man and had a big crush on him. I was hoping she would find comfort crying on the wide shoulders of her new love.

We took Jordanian Airlines to Amman. As we settled in our seats, I noticed that people around me were talking and laughing. That made me really mad. When the sun came out the morning after my father died, that also made me mad. I wanted to scream at the people on the plane, to tell them that my father had just died and that they should shut up. Instead, I asked the flight attendant if I could have the Jordanian newspapers. "Please, I need a copy of each." My heart dropped when I saw my father's pictures. All the newspapers were filled with announcements and editorials about his death. The sad reality of losing my father started to sink in. He was gone forever.

Exhausted, we arrived at my parents' home in the late afternoon. The house was packed with people, some I knew and others I didn't. My brother Ayman and sister Arwa and her family were already there, and so were many other relatives and friends who had come from various cities. To my utter surprise, what had not yet arrived was my father's body. The Czechoslovakian government had made all the necessary arrangements to send his body to the Amman airport, but the Jordanian government wouldn't hear of it. Their logic was that he left Jordan through the Syrian border and had to come back, dead or alive, via the same route. So, my father's body had to be sent by plane to Damascus, then to Amman, in an ambulance. My cousin Nabila drove my father's car behind the ambulance back to my parents' home.

Three days after my father's funeral, our home started to empty. My sister and brother went back to their cities, and so did other relatives. They all promised to come back for the *Arba'een,* a ceremony observed forty days after a person's death. Since my sister Suad and I lived so far away, we decided to stay with our mother until the Arba'een.

The Jordanian Writers Union planned to have a public Arba'een memorial for my father. They booked a large auditorium at the King Hussein Cultural Center, a government multifunction complex, and asked a few of my father's close friends, including Sheik Abdel Hamid al-Sayeh,[29] to help plan the memorial. Although Sheik Sayeh was a Muslim cleric, he and my socialist father loved and respected each other. Planning the memorial with my father's colleagues and friends was the most comforting and healing experience. While we came from different walks of life, we all wanted to have a memorial worthy of Baba, a memorial that would honor his public service and intellectual contributions.

A couple of days before the ceremony, my sister Arwa and brother Ayman came back. Dozens of my mother's relatives drove from Damascus and Beirut, and others flew from Cairo, Baghdad and Tunis. Politicians, activists and writers—including presidents of other Arab Writers Unions, many of whom were in Prague with my father—also came. My mother's home looked like a zoo, and we didn't know who was coming or going. People were sleeping in beds, on the couches and on the floor. We were overwhelmed with so many guests, but delighted with the outpouring of support.

The Arba'een memorial was scheduled for Monday, January 29, at four o'clock. On Sunday morning, the day before the memorial, my mother's friend Ne'mat called. Ne'mat never missed listening to local and national news, or reading all the daily newspapers.

"What happened? Why did you cancel the memorial?" Ne'mat asked.

"What are you talking about? We didn't cancel the memorial. We have dozens of guests from all over," I heard my mother say.

"What do you mean you didn't? There is an announcement in today's newspapers. Here let me read it: *With great regret, the Aamiry family and the Jordanian Writers Union apologize for having to cancel Mohammed Adib Aamiry's memorial service due to unusual circumstances.*"

"Ne'mat. I'm telling you, we didn't cancel. That can't be true!" screamed my mother.

"It's true, I have the newspaper in my hand."

My mother hung up the phone. Her face was so pale. She started crying.

"Mama, what's wrong?" I asked.

"I don't understand. Why does everything about your father, even when he is dead, have to be so complicated?"

I knew it. Sooner or later, my mother was going to criticize my father. Actually I was surprised it took her that long.

"What happened now?" I asked.

"Hand me today's paper, go to the store and get me a copy of all the others."

"Tell me, what's going on?"

"Just go," she said, almost yelling.

I ran to the store and bought every daily newspaper, including the English one. Sure enough, all had the same announcement. Every guest at the house had an opinion about what had happened and why, and what my mother should do about it. As we were pondering and accusing the Muslim Brothers, who hated my father, Sheik Abdel Hamid al-Sayeh and Salem Nahas from the Writers Union appeared at our door.

"These bastards," said the Sheik, "they have no shame."

We were all shocked to hear this dignified Muslim cleric use such language.

"Who are they?" I asked.

"The Jordanian government. Who else?"

"I'll call the newspapers to find out who placed the ads," said my brother Ayman.

"I already did, but they won't tell me," Salem said.

"We have all these guests from out of town, and we're expecting many locals to come, including Jordanian officials," Mother said, then she started crying.

People circled my mother, comforting her, promising to fix it.

"The only thing we can do is to purchase new ads stating that the cancellation announcement was in error and that the memorial ceremony will be as planned, same time, same place. We ought to do this right now if it's to appear in tomorrow's newspapers," said Arwa.

All of a sudden my mother composed herself and told Arwa, "Go ahead and place the counter-announcement."

Arwa quickly drafted a couple of lines and started to call the newspapers to find out who paid for the cancellation announcement and to place the new one. No one would answer her question, but all promised to correct the mistake. As soon as Arwa was done, my mother took over. Frantically she started calling high government officials who knew and respected my father, asking them to help her find out who placed the cancellation announcement. By two o'clock, the end of the workday for government agencies, we knew we were not going to get any answers.

All afternoon our phone didn't stop ringing. People were calling to inquire about the cancellation. Meanwhile, my siblings and I were calling out-of-town guests to tell them that the memorial ceremony was not cancelled. I'm not sure if our calls created more confusion or not, since many had not heard about the cancellation. By the end of the day, exhausted, we all collapsed, hoping for a better tomorrow.

On Monday morning, I was awakened by my mother's dramatic scream: "*Welad al-haram*, these bastards!" I jumped up from my floor mattress, wondering what was going on now. Other guests came out of the bedrooms and gathered around my mother.

"What's wrong, Siham? Why are you screaming?" asked Aunt Nahida.

My mother held the newspaper, shaking it violently, "They didn't publish our announcement."

"Mama, don't panic. I'm sure other newspapers did," I said trying to comfort her.

I hurriedly put on some clothes, and ran, one more time, to the store to buy copies of all the other newspapers. None had the announcement. My mother became even more hysterical.

"This is awful, what are all these guests going to say?" screamed my mother.

"Who cares about who says what. Stop screaming or you'll die from a heart attack just like your husband," said my aunt.[30]

We all tried to calm my mother down, running around, making her coffee, bringing her rose water, but she kept crying, which really broke my heart. She and my father argued all the time, and she always resented being married to him, but I guess she must have loved him. Or, despite her courage, she was so fearful of the unknown.

Realizing that the government was not going to allow us to have the public memorial, we decided to ask people to come to my parents' home. Ayman called Salem Nahas and asked him to help us contact out-of-town guests and inform them about the change. He also asked Salem to send a few union members to meet my sister Suad and me at the auditorium entrance where the memorial was supposed to be held. We wanted to greet and apologize, in person, to those who might not have heard about the cancellation. Arwa and Ayman were to stay with my mother to be sure she didn't totally lose it.

When we arrived at the auditorium, we were surprised to find dozens of policemen blocking all of the entrances to the building. We were ordered to leave, although standing there was by no means illegal.

"All we want is to apologize to people about the cancellation," I said.

"We'll tell them. But you need to leave," said one officer.

No matter how much we pleaded with them, they wouldn't allow us to stay. We had no choice but to head back home. On the way back, I begged people not to tell my mother about what happened. I wasn't sure she could handle one more insult, or if I could handle one more of her meltdowns.

The guests started to gather at our house. By four in the afternoon our home was about to burst from so many people. Those who were scheduled to speak at the memorial said a few words, as did others. We sat there reminiscing about my father, telling stories and jokes about him and cursing the Jordanian government, who, after all his service, would not allow us to publicly honor him. But in many ways, I wasn't sad that the memorial was cancelled. The intimacy and the warmth of that evening could not have been matched. Had my father been able to talk to us from his grave he would have said, "You should have known better. As my dear friend Sheik Sayeh said, they are just bastards." And I would have fainted hearing my extremely proper and polite father uttering such an obscene word.

**My father six months before he died,
Amman, 1978.**

22. MY FATHER FROM JAFFA

Washington, DC, March 1991

My father was a socialist and an Arab nationalist. He was from the Mediterranean city of Jaffa—"the Bride of the Sea," as Jaffaites call it. When we were children, my father used to tell us: "You're the lucky generation. You'll see peace return to Palestine. You'll see Palestinians go back to their homeland. You'll be able to go to Jaffa where I was born and raised." He would pause for a few seconds, then say in a sad voice, "I know it'll happen one day, but I doubt it will happen in my lifetime."

"Please Baba, don't say that. You should be more optimistic," I would beg.

"Maybe I should. But I should also be realistic. When it comes to Palestine, I've my fair share of disappointment."

My father talked a lot about Jaffa. To him it was the most beautiful place on earth. He talked about its warm clean shores where he swam almost daily with his friends.

"In Jaffa," he would tell us, "there was always plenty of fruit. We used to buy a full camel load of oranges or watermelons for only one shilling."

Baba told us many stories about his childhood. Stories about his home and school. He told us how much he liked being a student and a boy scout. He claimed he was good in every subject, and was always the first in his class.

I, who was not particularly good in school, would tease him saying, "All the parents I know claim to be the first in their class. I wonder who was last?" Baba had vowed more than once to prove his

My father (*second from right*), **in the Palestinian
Boy Scouts, Jaffa, around 1924. (Courtesy IPS
Photo Archive, Ramallah.)**

claim, but he never did. Music was the only subject he would admit
he wasn't good at: "I tried more than once to learn how to play a
musical instrument, but I couldn't. I just don't have a musical ear."

Baba yearned for Jaffa and for his aging blind uncle Deeb, his
only relative left in Palestine. In 1970, the Israeli government was
"kind" enough to grant my father a permit to visit. It was his first
visit since 1948, and as it turned out, it was also his last.

It was a painful return. His uncle, who had raised him after
his father died when he was only ten years old, was no longer
living. His school was totally demolished. The Jewish family who
was living in his home pushed him away as he tried to tell them
he once lived there. They threatened to call the police if he didn't
leave. So he left his home and he left Jaffa, trying to hide his tears.

My father cried every time he told the story of his visit. I cried
too. I was not used to seeing my father cry. In my culture, men
do not cry, they just burst into anger or drop dead from repressed
pain, like my father, who ultimately died from a severe heart attack.

My world has never been the same.

I loved my Baba. He had a beautiful smile.

The morning news confirmed that Iraq had been totally destroyed. At least 250,000 Iraqis were killed. The Kuwait Ambassador to the US appeared on the television screen. He was thanking President Bush and the American army and the new world order for liberating his country. I felt I was about to burst from anger. The pain was too much to endure. I was afraid I was about to die from a heart attack, just like my father did.

Then I remembered when Baba let me in on one of his secrets. He told me:

"After the 1967 war and our humiliating defeat, I loaded my gun, locked the door of my study and was ready to kill myself. I just couldn't take the loss of Jerusalem and the rest of Palestine. What stopped me, were you, my children. I thought, 'My children are still too young to understand. I can't do this to them.'"

If my father were still alive, I wondered, would he be able to deal with this new world order? Would he be able to deal with the destruction of Iraq? Or would he say, "My children are adults now. They can handle my death." And I caught myself thinking, *Thank God my father is not alive…thank God my father is not alive…*

23. My Jerusalem

In transit, winter 2017

Jerusalem is like no other city in the world. It has its own colors, sounds and smells. I love the walled city—the Old City. I love the way Palestinian peasant women guard their niches. With their tanned faces, even in February, they fill the entrance to the city. They've been coming here, day in and day out, for generations, bringing their fruit, vegetables and other produce to market. They bring their children, too. Sitting on the sidewalks, their colorful embroidered dresses and large, bright pink-and-blue wool scarves celebrate their presence and protect them from the wind and cold.

I love the noise of the crowded city, the vendors, the streams of men in their kifayah headdresses, and the boys and girls playing. I love the smells of freshly baked bread, the olives, the spices and the delicious zaatar. And I love the blend of all these colors and scents. They invite me to experience my senses in a unique way. They give me a feeling of security and reaffirm my belonging to my childhood city.

Whenever I visit Palestine, I can't wait to get to Jerusalem. My sister Suad, who lives in Ramallah and is the only connection we still have to our homeland, doesn't understand why I don't want to visit other cities. She keeps telling me, "There are other beautiful places in Palestine."

"Maybe tomorrow," I reply. "Today I want to go to Jerusalem."

Tomorrow comes, and I go back to Jerusalem. I hurry there as if I'm going to meet my first date.

In East Jerusalem, I walk the streets of Sheikh Jarrah, my childhood neighborhood. The scent of jasmine draws me along, always reminding me of the small tree my mother brought from Damascus and planted in our front yard. Our home somehow still holds my earliest memories: the birth of a goat on a warm spring day; the joy on my father's face at giving me a baby lamb; playing doctor with the boy next door; helping our neighbor Amo Adli, my first adult friend, feed his pet birds and take care of them; meeting for the first time one of my father's relatives, his brother Amo Omar.

I head to the Old City. Like a ritual, I always enter through Damascus Gate. There is something majestic about this gate, although I was almost shot right there. That was in 1989, when I came to participate in an international peace march. Peace, as well as the march, were shattered as Israeli bullets filled the place. I was very frightened. An Italian woman lost her eye. My heart ached for her. She came all the way from Rome chanting peace; she left with one eye.

My first stop in the Old City is usually the falafel stand. But if I manage to get to the city early enough, I go instead to the ancient pastry shop, Zalatemo Sweets. There I get *mutabaq*, a paper-thin dough stuffed with cheese and honey. My father used to bring us to Zalatemo for breakfast on Friday mornings, only an hour's drive from Amman. Back then, I was fascinated by the place more than the food. The people who worked there looked as ancient as their shop. My father loved coming here on Fridays.

Then came 1967. Israel occupied the rest of Palestine, and we could not visit Jerusalem anymore. But in 1974, I married an Arab American, moved to Michigan and in 1980 became a US citizen. Thanks to my American passport, I once again could return to Palestine and to my

My scarf from Jerusalem.

childhood city. Occupied, annexed, suffocated by high-rise settlements, miraculously the colors, sounds and smells of the city remain Palestinian.

In the Old City I buy gifts, pottery and zaatar. I also buy an embroidered peasant's dress, along with a bright pink wool scarf—all so I can bring a few pieces of Jerusalem, its beautiful colors and smells, back to my home in the US.

In America, I wear my beautifully embroidered dress. I wear it to fancy dinners, to big parties and special celebrations. In the grey of winter, I wear it with my pink scarf. I get so many compliments that I proudly say, "I bought it in Jerusalem. It is a traditional Palestinian dress. Women in my country still wear it."

With each trip though, what I am never able to bring back with me is a particular, familiar scent of jasmine. No matter how much I try, unlike me, it somehow resists adjusting to life in the new world.

As I travel now, I think more than ever about Jerusalem and Damascus, about all the cities of the Arab world I've lived in. I think of my hardworking parents, who are no longer here. My mother's free-spirited independence, the way she herself loved to travel and explore, her fearless encouragement to reject the assumption that men were more intelligent or competent than myself, and her belief that I could be whoever I wanted to be, could accomplish whatever I set my mind to; my father's honesty and integrity, his insistent compassion, his sense of justice, of responsibility and service to others. I can gratefully see that these gifts from my parents have kept me company and given me strength through all the darkest times of challenge and defeat. And I wonder if this familiar scent of jasmine I am always yearning and looking for has been with me—part of me—all along.

Glossary

ace: green branches

ahlan wa sahlan: welcome.

Ahlan wa sahlan, sharraftona: Welcome, you honor us with your presence.

akaber: classy

alhamidulillah: thank God

al-kaser (literally, the palace): the name given to two quarters on the third floor of my grandfather's house, each one including a very large room and a smaller one

Al salam alaykum: May peace be upon you (traditional greetings used by both Muslims and Christians in the region).

Allah kareem: God is generous.

Allah ma'ek ya binti: May God be with you, my daughter.

Allah yefrejha: May God ease the situation.

Allah yehmeek ya ibni: May God protect you, my son.

Allah la yesamhek ya: May God never forgive you.

Allah ma'akum...Allah yehmeekum: May God be with you...may God protect you.

Allah yosturha: God help us.

amo: uncle, father, brother, but also used as a term of respect

Beeti beetac: My home is your home.

Beit Jido: Grandfather's House

Bism Allah al Rahman al Rahim [Bism Allah al Rahman al Raheem]: In the name of God the merciful.

Bism Allah...ya lateef: In the name of God, the kind.

burma: a desert made of very fine fried wheat noodles wrapped around pistachios and sweetened with honey

chai: tea

dahleeze: a long corridor

diar: courtyard

diwan: a long sofa with no back or arms

eib: shameful

eid: holy day

franka: in my grandfather's house, a second-floor room used mostly as a living room in the winter

Fal yasqut Helf Baghdad: Down with the Baghdad Pact.

habibi: sweetheart (boy)

habibti: sweetheart (girl)

hammam: a bath and a bathroom, it also is used to refer to a public communal bathhouse

Inshallah: God willing.

Ismallah: In the name of God.

istiqbal: a gathering, usually for women

Jido: Grandfather

kabbad and *narinje*: citrus fruits

ka'ek: bread with sesame seeds; also used for special kind of sweet desserts

kahlo: uncle

kahlto: aunt

kahwa: coffee

karawyeh: caraway pudding, especially served to guests when a child is born

kartooneh: cardboard (my mother used it to refer to a university certificate)

kibbeh nayee (raw kibbeh): a dish made of very lean raw lamb or beef, mixed with cracked wheat, graded onion and spices (salt, pepper, allspice, and sometimes cardamom)

Kheir Inshallah: Good news, I hope.

Kul sana wa inta salem: Happy holidays, to address males.

Kul sana wa inti salmeh: Happy holidays, to address females.

kussa: zucchini

Ma'as salameh: Goodbye

Mabrook: Congratulations

Mafi mettel elbanat: There is nothing like girls.

maleessah: lemon verbena

marhaba: hi

mukhabarat: Jordanian intelligence

nabet ya fool: boiled beans

qa'ah: hall

Nushkur Allah: Thank God

salamaat: greetings

shukran ya ibni: thank you, son.

suma'a: reputation

sura: a Quran chapter verse

tarbush: fez

tawleh: backgammon

taza ka'ek: Fresh sesame bread

Teta: Grandmother

uba'ab: wooden slippers

wa alaykum al salam: and peace may be upon you

waddu: a washing ritual before praying

waleh: hey, you

wallah: I swear

welad al-haram: these bastards

Ya Arwa ya habibti: Arwa, sweetheart

ya binti: my daughter

Ya eib alshoom alaykum: Shame on you.

ya ukhti: my sister

Yallah: Come on.

youm al-hammam: bath day

youm al-waqfa: the day before Eid al-Fitr or Eid al-Adha

zagrting: ululating

zakzek: squeaking noise

NOTES

1   The American Junior College for Women (AJCW) was first established in 1835 by American Presbyterian missionaries as the American
School for Girls. When my mother attended the college in the early
1920s, its name was changed to AJCW. Since then, the name of the
college has changed several times. When I attended it from 1962 to
1963, its name was Beirut College for Women (BCW). In 1975 the
college began admitting men. Today, it is the Lebanese American
University.

2   *Libyoot asrar.* An Arabic proverb meaning "Homes have their own
secrets."

3   Huna al-Quds: This Is Jerusalem was a British-run radio station with
Arabic, Hebrew and English sections. It was located in West Jerusalem
before 1948.

4   Before the creation of the State of Israel in 1948, Jerusalem was one
city. In 1948, the western part of the city fell under Israeli control and
became known as West Jerusalem. The other part became known as
East, or Arab, Jerusalem.

5   My grandfather's house was built in 1737.

6   In 1949, when I was five years old, my family settled in the Sheikh
Jarrah neighborhood in East Jerusalem. We rented the middle flat from
the Muhtadi family, who lived on the third floor. On the first floor
lived a family with a Palestinian father and a blond German mother.
My brother Ayman was born that year. When I visited the house in
1996, its three floors were occupied by the Turkish Consulate.

7   As a sign of respect, the young are expected to call unrelated adults
Amo (Uncle) and Khalto (Auntie).

8   The Muslim holiday of Eid al-Adha honors God's timely interven-
tion of sending Abraham a lamb to sacrifice instead of sacrificing
his son Ishmael. Traditionally, Muslims commemorate the holiday by
slaughtering a lamb, giving one-third to a needy neighbor or a friend,
one-third to the poor, and cooking the rest for the holiday feast.

9   Unlike with my mother's family, I did not enjoy the same intimate
relationship with my father's family during my early childhood. My
paternal grandfather died when my father was only ten. His mother
and his one sister died before he got married. My father lost touch
with his two siblings, as well as his extended family, during the chaotic expulsion of Palestinians in 1948. However, he was able to find

his brother and sister, and to help them move to Amman, where we ultimately settled in 1951.

10 Palestinians refer to the 1948 creation of the State of Israel as the Nakba (the Disaster). Close to 850,000 Palestinians lost their homes and became refugees. They were never able to go back or claim their lost properties despite many UN resolutions that granted them the right of return.

11 It took me a while to realize that my father, in fact, did have his own extended family. His uncle's family and a few cousins ultimately settled in Jordan after Aunt Naima did. Others settled in different parts of the world; some I never met.

12 Aunt Naima, to whom I became very attached, gave birth to two more boys. All of her eight children, except one, graduated from college; at least half went on to graduate school. In the 1970s, she took her youngest five children and moved on her own to Cairo, where life was less expensive and college education was free. Once they all graduated, she moved back to Amman.

13 A game played on a dark checkered cloth with metal pieces in two colors (one color for each player) and six small shells, instead of dice, to get the score.

14 I don't know when Khalo Rashad told his first family about his second marriage, or when he totally moved in with his second wife, who I never met. Pearl, his first wife, ultimately went back to England. She got her revenge by writing a book about how rotten a husband he was.

15 In the mid-1970s, long after my grandparents' deaths, my two aunts, Suad and Nahida, along with Fawziyeh, left my grandfather's house and moved to a smaller "modern" apartment in Beirut. It was age and not modernity that caught up with them. They could no longer take care of the aging Jabri home. My jido's home was deserted for a few years, but thanks to my cousin Raed, the home was reopened as the Jabri Restaurant (www.jabrihouse.com).

16 Ghar, or laurel, soap is also known as Aleppo soap. Its primary ingredients are laurel oil and olive oil.

17 Arabic for "holiday," the word "eid" is used by both Muslims and Christians in reference to religious holidays like Christmas, Easter, Eid al-Adha, and Eid al-Fitr. It is also used for other non-religious days like Mother's Day (Eid al-Um), or birthdays (Eid Milad).

18   The years 1955 and 1956 were ones of protest and political upheaval in Jordan. It was a time when England sought to maintain its dominance over its previous colonies through various treaties, among them the Baghdad Pact, an alliance that included Jordan, Iraq and Turkey.

19   The unyielding popular pressure throughout Jordan, which was met with police violence and brutality, ultimately prevented the Jordanian government from joining the pact. High school students joined the demonstrations on a regular basis and often managed to get middle-school students to be part of the protest, as well. This was my initiation to political protest—soon after I celebrated my eleventh birthday.

20   When I was growing up, people in Jordan protested a lot. There were always demonstrations taking place, some bigger than others. The protesters would descend, at the same time, from Amman's seven hills that surrounded downtown, and gather in the square in front of the Grand Husseini Mosque. The final destination of each demonstration, however, depended on the nature of the protest. Sometimes it would be Parliament, the Prime Minister's office or a political prison. Other times we marched to the British, French or Saudi embassies. With the escalation of the Vietnam War in the 1960s, the US embassy was added to the list.

21   "Ma Yatluboho al-mustameo'un," "listeners' requests," a popular music program broadcast by many radio stations, played songs requested by people via phone or letter.

22   Huna al-Qahera: This Is Cairo was an Egyptian radio station that was very popular throughout the Arab world during Nasser's presidency.

23   *Lateefeyeh* refers to a religious ritual and is derived from the word *lateef,* or kind, referring in this case to God, the Kind.

24   *Basha* (also *Pasha*) is a Turkish word used for a high official position in the Turkish Empire. Its more popular use refers to elite or upper-class status. My mother used to call my younger brother Ayman *Pasha* as a term of endearment.

25   My mother used to work at the print shop my father and three of his friends bought in the early 1950s. They were hoping to publish a progressive newspaper, but they never got around to it. Eventually my mother bought out the partners and turned it into a commercial print shop. My mother was the first woman in Jordan who owned her own business in downtown Amman and managed an all-male staff. She worked there until her early seventies. She was unable to keep up with the rapidly changing technology that altered the face of the printing business.

26 Hizb al-Shaab, People's Party was a nationalist Syrian political party that was active in the 1950s and 1960s.

27 Sunni and Shi'a are the two largest branches of Islam.

28 In the US, away from my parents' pressure, I enrolled in a PhD program at Wayne State University. "This is the best news we could ever have," said both of my parents. I graduated in 1981. My mother was happy and proud. Sadly, my father was no longer living. My parents' mission to see their children highly educated had come to fruition.

My sister Arwa got her first PhD in cognitive psychology from University of Louisville, Kentucky, and her second PhD from the University of Florida, in clinical health psychology. She taught at the University of Jordan from 1973 to 2013. She currently works as a therapist at her own clinic in Amman. She has two beautiful daughters, Diala and Alma.

My sister Suad resides in Ramallah, Palestine. She graduated with a PhD in architecture from the University of Edinburgh. In 1991, she founded the nonprofit organization RIWAQ for Architectural Preservation (www.riwaq.org). Currently, she dedicates her time to writing, and is the author of numerous books including the infamous *Sharon and My Mother-in-Law*.

My brother Ayman currently resides in Amman. He graduated from the American University of Beirut, with a degree in political science. He worked for a few years with my mother in her print shop, then persued a diplomatic career with the Jordanian Ministry of Foreign Affairs. He worked with the Jordanian mission to the UN for a few years, as well as at the Jordanian Embassy in Washington, DC, in the early 1990s, when I was also living there. It was then that I got to know my brother as an adult and we formed a special bond despite our continued political differences.

29 Cleric Abdel Hamid al-Sayeh was the Supreme Judge in Jerusalem. He was the first Palestinian to be expelled from Jerusalem after 1967, when Israel occupied East Jerusalem, the West Bank and Gaza.

30 My mother continued to work in her print shop well into her early seventies. She died in 2005 at age eighty-two.

ACKNOWLEDGMENTS

To my countless friends, I am blessed to have so many of you, who for more than twenty-some years kept telling me, "You are a good storyteller"…"This is too important"…"You should put it on paper." Thank you.

Initially I started drafting some of these stories in the mid-1990s when I took a one-year sabbatical from my job. While I gave up writing to pursue a new career, my family, friends and husband never gave up on me. It took me almost twenty years, and an official retirement, finally to be able to sit down and write this book. But it also took an army of friends who kept nagging me to write.

First and foremost, I want to express my heartfelt gratitude to my husband Noel Saleh, who repeatedly read every single word of this book; who critiqued, edited and brainstormed with me on so many evenings and weekends. I truly appreciate your patience, thoughtful comments and wisdom. I am especially grateful to my sister Suad, niece Diala and brother-in-law Salim Tamari for reading the manuscript and for their priceless feedback; to my sister Arwa, who was always ready to help me with fact checking of events, dates and names; to my brother Ayman for scanning and sending family photos; and to my niece Alma who kept pleading with me to go back to writing.

I am especially indebted to my two late friends, Jeff Rosen Karaman, who kept telling me "you should go back to writing," and Diane Binson, who read and commented on most of my writing. Sadly, they did not have a chance to see this work come to fruition. I want to acknowledge my friends Jane Power, the first to edit my very early writing; Angelita Espino, not only for reading and editing but also for her unwavering encouragement; Anne Berggren, and Zilka Joseph for their excellent remarks; Kirsten Terry-Murphy, for scanning the photos of this book, and Kim Silarski and Fay Saad for bailing me out whenever I was in a crunch.

I am very grateful to my dear friends Barbara Kessler and Holly Arida for reading the manuscript and giving me their invaluable critique and advice; to my friend and colleague Greta Anderson Finn for her comments and excellent copyediting; my friend and writer pal Evelyn Alsultany; the Ann Arbor Area Writers Group at Nicola's

Books—your honest comments, suggestions and reassurance made me a better writer; to Paula Hajar and Amani Elkassabany, whose thinking helped to clarify this memoir's final form, and to all those who read the manuscript and gave me their endorsement. Thank you.

To all my other friends, who read some of these vignettes, and pushed me to keep going, I cannot thank you enough for your love and support. I am so fortunate to have you in my life. As the saying goes, "It takes a village to raise a child"; well, it took my whole family and a village of friends to write this book. It would take pages to list all of them.

Last but not least I am beholden to the staff at Interlink Publishing: Meredith Madyda for her commitment to this project and editorial work on its content, Pam Fontes-May for her insightful design work, and Whitney Sanderson for her careful proofreading of the manuscript.

My special gratitude to publisher Michel Moushabeck for sustaining a tenacious, independent small press that creates a space for so many voices, and to editor John Sobhiea Fiscella for his patient, wonderful work helping me pull all the pieces of this book together so my voice could be heard.

ABOUT THE AUTHOR

Dr. Anan Ameri is an activist, scholar, author and founder of the Arab American National Museum (AANM). She is also the co-founder of many progressive political and cultural coalitions in the US. For more than forty years, Ameri has been driven by her passion for culture and history. She is a recognized leader who enjoys extensive relationships with the Arab American communities in Michigan and throughout the nation. Ameri is also known to the broader community as a lifelong advocate for social justice.

Ameri has served as acting director of the Institute for Jerusalem Studies in Jerusalem; visiting scholar at Harvard University's Center for Middle Eastern Studies; and was the founding director and national president of the Palestine Aid Society of America. Prior to immigrating to the US in 1974, she worked as a program director at Jordanian Television and a researcher at the Palestine Research Center in Beirut, Lebanon.

Anan Ameri is author of numerous books and articles, including *Telling Our Story: The Arab American National Museum* (2007, AANM) and a series of four booklets, all published in 2010 by the *AANM: Monotheistic Religions; Islam and Muslim Americans; Arab Americans: An Integral Part of American Society*; and *The Arab World*. She is co-author of *Arab Americans in Detroit: A Pictorial History* (2001, Arcadia) and *Etching Our Own Image: Voices from the Arab American Art Movement* (2007, Cambridge Scholars Press). She is also contributing author and co-editor of *The Arab American Encyclopedia* (2000, UXL) and *Daily Life of Arab Americans in the 21st Century* (2011, Greenwood Press).

Ameri was born in Damascus, Syria and grew up in Amman, Jordan. She received her BA in sociology from the University of Jordan, in Amman; her MA in sociology from Cairo University in Egypt; and her PhD in sociology from Wayne State University in Detroit.

Dr. Ameri is the recipient of numerous local and national awards in recognition of her work within the Arab American community, as well as society at large. In 2016, she was inducted into Michigan Women's Hall of Fame.